The Girl Who Had No Enemies
and the
MaN WhO HaTeD WoMeN

DENNIS PATRICK FLEMING

Printed in the United States of America
First Printing, 2012
ISBN: 1467993573
ISBN-13: 978-1467993579

Author's Note

This book is a memoir, more specifically a literary true crime memoir. It is based on my best efforts to remember personal experiences. I have gathered information on some people, conversations, and events from court documents, interviews, research, journals, press accounts, and the memories of friends and acquaintances. I've done my best to represent events and circumstances as they happened. To protect the identity of some individuals, such as witnesses, their names and identifying characteristics have been changed. No person or event has been fabricated or condensed.

For Mickey

Mary Michelle Fleming's last, courageous act raised an alarm, which ultimately led to the capture of her killer. Her actions that fateful day saved the lives of many innocent people who might have crossed paths with serial killer Anthony J. LaRette Jr. had he not been apprehended less than two weeks later. I dedicate this book to families of murder victims. My deepest wish is that you will find comfort in my struggle. To readers who have not lost a loved one through a purposeful, violent act, my wish is that you will see this story as a cautionary tale.

Acknowledgments

The first person I must thank is my friend, writer and producer Roberta "Bobbie" Lautenschlager, for introducing me to writer-producer Diana Ossana during the annual screenwriters conference in Austin, Texas. Ms. Ossana encouraged me to write the story about the impact of the loss of my baby sister as a memoir and not as a screenplay.

This book would not have been possible without the encouragement and help of Kathleen Finneran, whose talent, intellect, and beautiful memoir, *The Tender Land* (Houghton Mifflin), continue to inspire me.

My first editor, writer/editor Gary Anderson (ABC Iowa Writing & Editing), made the editing process fun.

Eileen Dugan gave of her valuable time in guiding me in making correct editorial decisions.

I can't thank Mary J. Schirmer enough for her keen editor's sense and incredible attention to detail. Working with Mary made the process enjoyable and educational.

A special thanks to scholar, video artist, and friend, R D Zurick, for his belief in me as an artist.

Thanks to my agent, Peter Riva, who believed in my abilities and encouraged me to develop my talent.

This book would have never arrived in this configuration without Peter's enthusiasm.

To my children, Megan, Sean, and Patrick, and my grandson, Jayden, all of whom pulled me away from my writing time. I don't regret one moment of it.

And finally, to my wife, Kathy, whose patience, support, and love enabled me to fulfill my dream of acquainting others with the beautiful sister my family will always cherish. Kathy, I love you.

Part I
Love and Anguish

You become responsible, forever, for what you have tamed. You are responsible for your rose.
From "The Little Prince and the Fox" by Antoine de Saint-Exupery

My youngest sister, Mickey, has been eighteen for more than thirty years now. She was born Mary Michelle Fleming on December 8, 1962. December 8 is the Catholic Church's feast of the Immaculate Conception. It celebrates the day an angel told the Virgin Mary that she was conceived without original sin. It is a holy day of obligation and mandates attendance at Mass. Deeply Catholic, Mom honored the Church by naming her youngest daughter Mary. It never occurred to me that early each December we were attending church on Mickey's birthday, but I guess that's because we didn't call her Mary.

We nicknamed our baby sister *Mickey* because of her middle name, Michelle. Her first name was just too holy, too church-like. The name Mickey was cute and less foreboding than the name of Jesus' mother. We were Mickey Mouse fans, and our little sister was small, like a tiny mouse, so it made sense to call her Mickey. She had curly blonde hair and hazel blue eyes like the rest of us. She made us a family of ten, but for me, she *was* the family.

She was the youngest, the baby of the family, and the most fragile. Whenever she got hurt—anything from a routine boo boo to a broken collarbone at three—her injury seemed worse than if it had happened to any of us.

When the unthinkable happened to her, it robbed from each of us the very concept of hope for happiness, and it drove into us a deep sorrow that made sadness enviable, while forcing love to cede to hatred a position of supremacy in our lives. A feeling, pure, and as powerful as the love I felt witnessing my first child enter the world, seeing her face for the first time—a feeling *that* powerful crystallized like a black diamond in my heart—I had to kill a man.

Kansas, October 1, 1951: Anthony "Tony" Joseph LaRette Jr. is born. The only son of Anthony Joseph LaRette Sr. and his wife Gertrude, Tony is dyslexic and has difficulty with math and spelling. At age six, the boy grabs an ungrounded wire on a trailer hitch. The shock hurls him to the ground, knocking him unconscious and breaking several of his teeth. Tony begins experiencing auditory hallucinations. He has trouble falling asleep at night because he hears a voice chanting, "Burma Shave," the name of a popular shaving lotion.

In 1967, Mickey was only four and had not yet entered kindergarten. I was seventeen and we lived on the outskirts of St. Charles, Missouri, a town of 60,000, thirty-five miles west of St. Louis. Mom and Dad had grown to hate each other and fought all the time.

She once told me that, shortly after they married, she realized she'd made a mistake, but she couldn't leave him. As a union electrician with an excellent blue-collar salary, he provided good income for the growing family—when he worked.

Six children into their marriage, Dad lost the Democratic Party primary for state representative. He'd expected to win big, but the results were just the opposite and they crushed him. The humiliation drove him into a whiskey bottle, where he stayed for the rest of his life. I couldn't understand why Mom wouldn't leave him. He beat and berated her in front of us. She seldom stood up to him, and when she did, she paid for it with bruises and broken bones. I finally realized that Mom couldn't go against her faith and file for a divorce. The Catholic Church wouldn't allow it.

She was stuck with him.

I'd grown used to their screaming and fighting, the guns and broken bones, but I could remember a time when we were a real family, and I'd felt loved. Mickey and Susie, who was a year older than Mickey, had never known life without our parents' lunacy.

The night I left home for good, Dad was drunk and pounding Mom's chest trying to stop her heart. I'd decided to let him kill her and get himself thrown in jail. I was in the den trying to ignore them, but they woke Mickey and Susie. Mom's desperate pleas and Dad's threats to put her into the ground scared the girls into the kitchen where they stood facing me, while cowering against the ruckus behind them. Little Mickey, her eyes pleading for me to do something, was clutching her pillow like a life preserver and shivering hard as if she were cold. She jumped each time she heard a punch land with a thump behind her.

I rushed into the living room and grabbed Dad by his thick hair and belt. I rammed him headfirst through the sliding glass below a large picture window that faced the front yard. He took a deep breath and slowly sat up in the shattered glass, as Mom knelt beside him and checked him over. I waited long enough to see he wasn't bleeding badly before I left. I didn't want the police chasing me.

I swore that one day I'd get my little sisters out of there, but I never did. I was too busy trying to forget I had a family. And though I didn't follow Mickey's life closely after that, she had a special place in my heart. There was something between us that I couldn't explain—something I didn't sense with my other siblings. When I *did* think about my family, good thoughts about them, I found myself thinking of Mickey.

St. Petersburg, Florida: A baseball bat crack to eight-year-old Tony LaRette's left temple, during a neighborhood baseball game, renders him unconscious for about ninety minutes. He begins to wet the bed after that and urinates in his clothes in public

Several times over the next two weeks, he awakens lost and frightened miles from home.

Sweating profusely and salivating, he exposes himself to a woman, a St. Petersburg police detective, and he tries to tear off her clothes.

Tony is taken into custody and transferred to Mound Park Hospital where Alfred Koenig, M.D., of Psychiatric Associates Koenig-Holtzman examines him and administers an electroencephalography (EEG) test. Diagnosis: psychomotor epilepsy. Prescription: phenobarbital and vitamins.

I spent a couple of years trying to find myself in experiments with various psychedelic drugs, and wound up in Texas living on a diet of milk and peanut butter and sleeping in my beat-up '53 Chevy. I needed a way out of that life, so in November 1970 I enlisted in the Marine Corps, just after the peak of the Vietnam War, and right before Mom divorced Dad.

Joanie, three years older than me, said Mom finally found a priest who told her what she needed to hear—divorce was a sin, but Jesus had died for our sins, and God would surely forgive a woman who divorced her husband to escape the repeated beatings and humiliations that were tearing her family apart.

So Mom took Mickey and Susie and moved into a clean, peaceful neighborhood.

But Dad found her and continued to bother her for years, slashing her tires, sending nasty letters to her boss, and making crank phone calls to the house. Mom and the girls never knew when he would show up drunk, but he eventually grew tired of it all and felt guilty. He'd take the girls on holiday and birthday shopping sprees, spending far more on them than he could afford on his Social Security and union pension checks. Susie and Mickey always looked forward to those day trips with Dad.

The Marine Corps granted me a thirty-day leave after I graduated from boot camp in San Diego, California. I was on my way to a technical school at the naval air station in Jacksonville, Florida, so I stopped off to see the family, and Mom picked me up at the airport.

On the drive home through the cold February night, I told her I'd cleaned up my act during boot camp and discovered that my mind had survived my experiments with psychedelics in the '60s. My test scores had been high, and I was grateful to her for providing as best she could, despite her difficulties with Dad.

She said she was proud of me; proud of how I'd grown into a man, but I felt awkward. Something was missing. I could see Mom loved me, but I wasn't feeling it. I told her I had forgiven her for cheating me out of insurance money, thousands of dollars, I'd received from a car accident when I was fifteen. It had left me with an ugly scar over my left eye, and after three plastic surgeries, I hadn't been able to close my eyelid completely. Some kids in high school called me *Cyclops* and a Marine Corps drill instructor called me *Clit* Eye.

Forgiving Mom was the right thing to do, but it couldn't erase six years of lies. We got home late. Susie and Mickey were asleep.

St. Petersburg, Florida: Even with drug therapy, Tony suffers one to three seizures per week. Dr. Alfred Koenig notes his patient hears voices, smells rotten cabbage, has severe headaches and flies into rages, perspiring profusely and ripping off his clothes. Patient awakens frightened in public places, wet in urine and frothing at the mouth. He exposes himself to older women and tries to choke them. At age nine, unprovoked and enraged, he attacks a woman at a skating rink, badly bruising her and breaking her nose. At eleven, Tony is admitted to Mound Park Hospital in St. Petersburg for six months of treatment until he is transferred to the Arizona State Hospital in Phoenix, where he remains until he is fourteen years old.

I was up "boot-camp early" the next morning, jumped into my red Marine Corps gym shorts, and went out for a three-mile run. I ran on a hard, uneven path along a residential construction site behind our house. A warm front had moved in during the night and left the morning clear, cool, and sunny.

About fifty yards out, I heard Mickey yelling, "Wait, Denny! I'll run with you!" She had taken a shortcut and was running toward me, thin as a stick, her dishwater-blonde ponytail bobbing from side to side and lashing about her shoulders. Like most eight-year-olds, she sprinted to catch up and wasted some of her long-run energy.

"Let me catch up," she said.

"Okay, but I'm not going to slow down," I said.

She was taking two steps for every one of mine, so I gradually, imperceptibly slowed the pace.

"I bet I can keep up with you," she said.

We were running behind several blocks of two-story homes in different stages of construction. We veered off the path and ran up and down large frozen mounds of bulldozed earth.

"Do you run every day?" she asked.

"I miss a day once in a while. Sometimes I run in combat gear."

"With your gun?"

"Marines call it a weapon."

"Can you shoot it?" she asked, facing away from me to hide her labored breathing. "Any time you want to?"

"I only practice. In case I have to fire it."

"Did you ever shoot anybody?"

"No, Mickey, and I'd only do that to protect someone. I'm like a policeman."

Tiny beads of sweat were already breaking out on her forehead. We both perspired easily.

"Promise me something," I said.

"What?"

"Any time you see Dad's been drinking, you gotta promise me you'll stay away from him."

"Well, yeah, I'm not stupid."

"I know you're not stupid, but if he's mad and drunk, promise you'll hide or leave the house. Okay? Promise me you'll do that."

"I will," she said.

I didn't have to explain it to her. She wasn't disappointed that we had a father who was a drunk. She'd never known him any other way.

We talked about women in the Marines, and I told her that her best shot at getting somewhere in life would be to go to college and find a career.

She managed to keep up with me for about a mile. When she grew tired, I told her that I had to keep going at the same pace. "It's part of my training," I said.

She finally gave up and went back to the house. I slowed down when I was well out of her sight.

Arizona State Hospital, Phoenix: Tony's EEG is abnormal and indicates possible left hemisphere localization. He exposes himself while on the anticonvulsant drug Mysoline. His case records are sent to Johns Hopkins Hospital in Baltimore for assessment. Conclusion: Patient suffers from temporal lobe seizure disorder accompanied by sexual arousal and inappropriate behavior during a confused state preceding post-seizure amnesia.

St. Petersburg, Florida: Tony wets his pants while participating in competitive roller skating—a sport in which he'd won trophies. A rink attendant calls him a freak, and Tony attacks his female skating partner, her brother, and a bystander. He goes home and masturbates in front of a neighborhood girl before he rips off her clothes and breaks her arm.

Mickey looked up to me because I had a definite path in my life beyond a job, marriage, and kids. No one else in the family could say that. My four brothers were out of shape and playing with drugs. Mike was twenty-seven and adrift in a world of alcohol and marital infidelity. Mark was twenty, a year younger than I was, and glided through life in a haze of pot and mushrooms. Kevin was eighteen. He and Brian, the youngest, had to choose the Army over jail sentences.

Boot camp had opened my mind and swept it clean, but it also filled me with so much propaganda that I assumed a different personality. I was Private Fleming, U.S.M.C. I walked upright with purpose in each calculated step and thought as a Marine thought—all logic—Marine logic. It would be months before I recognized a thought as my own, but Mickey saw the exterior, the closely cropped hair, the fit and clean-shaven man. I represented a different world to her.

During my four-year hitch in the Marines, I crisscrossed the country, moving among military bases in California, Florida, Arizona, and Washington, and then back to California. In 1972, I spent a year on the USS Forrestal aircraft carrier traveling around the Mediterranean Sea with more than 5,000 Marines, Navy men, and seventy jets.

I enrolled in my first college class, English 101, aboard ship. Georgetown University in Washington, DC had worked a deal with the government. Several professors had signed on for the cruise, and taught their respective courses. We were reading, and writing essays on, J. D. Salinger's *Catcher in the Rye* and Antoine de Saint-Exupery's *The Little Prince*. I had written several letters to Mickey telling her about how the little prince had loved "tamed" his special rose, and how much Mickey was like *my* special rose.

I had lost track of everyone in my family, except Mickey. She and I corresponded often that year. I sent her little dolls from Athens, Istanbul, and Barcelona. She loved the Greek dolls, girls wearing gowns under short vests of red, blue, and yellow; the satin Spanish models, in dresses trimmed in lace; and the male Turkish replicas in their tasseled fez hats.

In return, she sent me drawings she'd made with crayons and construction paper. I would sit on the edge of my bunk—deep in the bowels of 60,000 tons of metal— tired from the 12-hour-on, 12-hour-off work schedule and read each picture as if it were a love poem. They put an extra bounce in my step for days afterward.

Once, Mickey glued a piece of black construction paper onto the back of a wall calendar cover. She drew two pictures on white paper and glued them, one above the other. The top picture was of two hotdog-shaped butterflies floating in a blue sky. The butterdogs hovered on wings that were simply wider versions of their bodies, above a rounded patch of green and brown earth. She'd drawn both butterflies crudely, but it was clear which one represented me. I was about three times her size and green with yellow wings. Her butterfly was yellow with pink wings. She floated between me and a large brown tree with a cloud of green leaves. In the lower left corner, she had printed her initials in pencil, M.M.F. The smiley faces on the butterflies were radiant. I knew what she was trying to say. With me at her side, she could safely hover in the world.

The bottom picture was labeled the sugarplum tree. Mickey had drawn many purple balls on the tree limbs, and had written a poem with arrows pointing at two plums in particular.

"This is the sugarplum tree. That is you. This is me."

I felt the love crying out from her crude, yet colorful pictures. They pulled a smile from deep within me and took me away from my duties as an electrician, keeping our phantom fighter jets in the air. Nine years old—young, innocent, and delicate—she had focused all her energy on a picture depicting herself and one of her five brothers on a family tree. The sugarplums looked alike, but two were special. Twelve years between us didn't matter. We shared a feeling of being outsiders long before she could verbalize it.

Topeka, Kansas: The LaRette family relocates from St. Petersburg, Florida. Tony, aged sixteen, marries his first wife, Janis. She and Tony are in an auto accident the following year. Janis is killed, and Tony sustains a closed head injury. He continues to smell rotten cabbage, and experience grand mal seizures, violent muscle contractions, and loss of consciousness.

The following year, Tony is in a stupor when admitted to Stormont-Vail Hospital in Topeka for three days. He hears voices telling him he is sick and that people will hurt him. The voices tell him not to let people touch him. He produces a normal EEG during the next year's evaluation at the Menninger Foundation Sanitarium and Clinic. Based on this test result, he enlists in the United States Marine Corps and is sent to the Marine Corps boot camp in San Diego, California. During close order combat training, he suffers a series of seizures after a drill instructor beats him with a pugil stick. Private LaRette is discharged honorably for psychomotor epilepsy, auditory hallucinations, and erroneous enlistment.

After my honorable discharge from the Marine Corps, I married my first wife, a tall Southern California blonde named Charlene. I attended California State University at Fullerton and planned to graduate, but if I didn't count Dad's two-day visit the previous summer—a bungled con had made it necessary for him to get out of town for a while—I hadn't seen my family in four years. I was homesick.

Charlene had never lived anywhere except Southern California, but she understood that I needed to go home. I could finish my degree there, and we could always return. We sold almost everything and dragged the rest to Missouri in a rented trailer. I had made several calls to Mom before we left California, so Mom, Dad, and my seven siblings, should have known that Charlene and I were coming. I expected most of them to be waiting.

It was after midnight on a partly-cloudy, moonlit night when we drove into a city neighborhood of small bungalows set on ill-tended lawns of weeds and overgrown grass. We pulled up to the curb in front of Mom's two-bedroom frame house. The front lawn slanted upward ten yards from the uneven sidewalk to a large front porch with splintered columns and a sagging roof. Were it not for the light streaming through the screen door, you'd think no one was home.

One of my younger sisters, but I couldn't tell who, was waiting there alone, a small silhouette sitting on the porch steps high above the street. Before I could see her clearly, she ran down the stairs and jumped into my open arms, crying and burying her face in my shoulder. She was heavier than the last time I'd held Mickey four years ago. Mickey would be fourteen now, two years younger than Susie would be and still roughly the same size.

I didn't want to hurt Susie's feelings if I was wrong, so I took a chance and asked. "Are you Mickey or Susie?" She slumped in my arms for a moment, and then tightened her hold on me. I could sense her joy melting into disappointment and sadness.

"How can you ask me that, Denny?" she asked, pushing her forehead harder into my shoulder.

"I'm sorry, Mickey," I said, holding her tighter.

"How can you even doubt it's me?"

"I should have known better," I said, setting her down and breaking our embrace for an instant before she hugged me again.

Susie was spending the night at a girlfriend's house. Mom was asleep in her bedroom, and Mark was sleeping in his van in the backyard. At least he had come. The other five were busy somewhere.

We woke Mom and Mark, and we all sat in the kitchen and talked for an hour. I kept catching Mickey staring at me, but whenever I'd acknowledge her, she'd begin to cry and would leave the room. Mom kissed her new daughter-in-law on the cheek and then went back to bed.

Mickey was tired, but we talked about what she'd been up to. She was proud of her athletic skills. None of us boys had shown any interest in playing sports beyond middle school. All five had dropped out of high school and into the family paradigm of alcohol and marijuana abuse. Only Joanie—three years my senior—had graduated. Mickey played basketball, soccer, and softball —and was excellent at all three.

We talked about how Charlene and I had met. I thought Mickey would be jealous that I'd found someone else to receive all my affections, but she had matured, and she and Charlene hit it off well. Charlene and I slept on a sleeper sofa in the front room, and we woke late in the morning to find Mickey, her hands full of dolls I'd sent her, standing at the foot of the bed.

My homecoming reception disappointed Charlene, and over the next few years, she would form varying opinions about each family member. Yet, she never forgot the sight of me holding Mickey—and the love that passed between us.

Topeka, Kansas: At 21, Tony is sentenced to up to four years for pocket picking and then sent to the Kansas Department of Corrections. Dr. Nagaswamy of the Topeka Veterans Hospital notes that Tony has blackouts and abnormal perceptions of food. He smells rotten cabbage, has other hallucinations of disagreeable odors during seizures, experiences déjà vu, and endures involuntary physical reflexes. He wears his shoes on the wrong feet and retains no memory of it. The patient's attacks of sexual deviation are followed by intense fear before falling asleep. He awakens the next morning with amnesia. Diagnosis: temporal lobe epilepsy with rape relation secondary to uncal seizures, with psychomotor double epilepsy starting on the left lobe and spreading to the right.

For six months, neurologist Arthur R. Dick, M.D., of the Kansas University Medical Center, in Kansas City, Missouri, treats Tony for adjustment to anticonvulsants and then transfers him to the Topeka State Hospital.

Topeka, Kansas: During his three-month stay at the Topeka State Hospital Tony produces two abnormal EEG tracings that correlate with temporal lobe epilepsy and diffuse encephalopathy with "character disorder of hysterical/narcissistic exhibitionism".

My credits from California State transferred to the local University of Missouri campus, and I continued my studies in the sciences while working as a microbiologist for a toiletry and cosmetic company.

After work one Friday, I dropped in on one of Mark's summer parties. Mickey was there, and she had been crying. Booze was everywhere at Mark's shindigs, and pot made the rounds like hors d'oeuvres. Occasionally, they passed around psychedelics, amphetamines, and barbiturates. I saw a syringe once and immediately split. I had a no-tolerance policy on needles.

I usually drank more around my family than I did in other social situations, and the more I drank, the more I craved a cigarette. I'd quit after boot camp, but cigarettes and alcohol liked to hang out in me like old friends when they got the chance. More than three beers and you'd catch me lighting up—a Marlboro, if I could fine one. Mickey saw me and I quickly crushed my cigarette into an ashtray.

"Why are you smoking?" she asked.

"It's a sign that I've had too much to drink. What's wrong with you?" I asked.

"Mark. He thinks I'm a slut." Her face, reddened from crying, grew redder.

I put an arm around her and pulled her close. Mark would never have said something like that unless it was a joke.

"Have you been drinking?" I asked.

"I drank part of one beer, Denny," she said. "You know me."

"Well, what's this about?"

"My boyfriend wants to have sex. He says it's important to him, and he doesn't want to wait. I told him I'm not ready yet, and he got upset. When I asked Mark what I should do, he just laughed and asked what the big deal was."

I held her for a few moments, envious that she had gone to Mark first, yet grateful, because without thinking, I might have given her similar advice. I wasn't the best person to seek advice from about losing your virginity. I'd lost mine at thirteen to a friend's twelve-year-old sister. She and I did it one night in a baseball dugout in a park across the street from our house in Washington, Missouri. I got home just in time to see the Beatles live on the Ed Sullivan Show.

If Mickey had come to me first, I might have asked her how important the boy was to her. If he was so special that she didn't want to lose him, I might have encouraged her to give his request a second thought, and, of course, use protection. But since she'd gone to Mark first, I knew I could be unequivocal and support her—and save face.

"What does Mark think I am?" she asked.

"Mark's stoned," I said. "He's not thinking about it seriously. Besides, we can count Mark's successful relationships on one hand. Let's see...umm...nope, he hasn't had any, zero! See?"

She tried to fight it with a frown, but a smile spread up from her cheeks, and she laughed in spite of herself.

"You're the only one who knows when you're ready to have sex. Don't let Mark bother you," I said. When she left the party, she was happier than when she had come to me earlier. Things worked out that way for us.

I never developed the same kind of relationship with Susie that I had with Mickey. Susie's a giving, sympathetic person, yet she's also skeptical about life in general—an attitude I've never understood. Despite her skepticism, she's very accepting—almost to a fault, which has led her into some abusive relationships with men.

I thought I had a special relationship with Joanie until I realized that she had a way of making all of us feel special, and it made me jealous. I wondered how she could speak so highly of Mark, who was smoking so much dope, or of Brian, who had a chronic problem with alcohol. I understood how she admired Kevin for his common sense and stability. He and his wife, Lynn, started a pizza company that delivered movies on VHS tape well before DVDs and the Internet.

We all had a problem with Mike. He was a loyal friend and brother, and he would drop everything to help someone. But he had a skewed perspective on family. He had deserted his wife and four children, only returning now and then to pick up some of their welfare money. Mom cut him out of her will. Dad was more sympathetic and overlooked his firstborn's faults. Mike had been born premature and, in 1944, that was a dangerous situation. He spent his first few weeks in a hospital incubator, diapered in Dad's new handkerchiefs. He repeated the first grade and dropped out of high school after repeating the ninth. Dad assured us that he'd make amends for Mike's disinheritance by leaving him a disproportionately higher amount of money than the rest of us. I'd always thought Mike would be the first of the children to die—

and to die penniless—since his drug use in the 1960s had developed into a lifelong addiction.

Larned, Kansas: At age 22, Tony breaks into the home of a Ms. Hecker and rapes her. He is arrested and admitted to Larned State Hospital for pretrial evaluations. They conclude he has passive aggressive personality disorder with antisocial and sexual deviant features. He is found competent to stand trial, is convicted of rape, and receives a five- to twenty-year sentence in the Kansas State Reformatory in Hutchinson.

Karl K. Tarownick, M.D., from the Menninger Clinic describes Tony as having an infantile personality with immature physical features, poor judgment, and interpersonal relationship skills deficiencies. Tony, notes Dr. Tarownick, has difficulty controlling impulses, especially sexual ones, and a reduced frustration tolerance. An EEG yields a mildly abnormal reading.

A neurosurgeon confirms Tony's temporal lobe epilepsy. He is found to have familial hypercholesterolemia and unstable blood Dilantin levels which makes his seizures difficult to control. Tony suffers two 40-minute grand mal seizures while incarcerated.

I showed up one afternoon at one of Mickey's high school softball games. She was the catcher, and she was sweating from the extra gear she was wearing. When she introduced me to some of her teammates, the girls giggled and gushed and treated me as though I were a movie star. Apparently, someone had created a fan club for me.

Mickey's school held a teachers conference the next day. She had the day off, so we drove to the University of Missouri - St. Louis (UMSL). She wanted to sit in on one of my classes.

The UMSL campus was a pedestrian set of buildings in Normandy, near the St. Louis city limits. Unlike other schools whose letters are pronounced individually—UCLA, NYU, and USC—UMSL was pronounced as a word, Umzle. A campaign to replace that epithet with UM-St. Louis failed, and Umzle stuck, like gum under an old school desk.

On the way to the campus, Mickey became quiet and reflective.

"Can I say something that might sound crazy?" she asked.

"Sure," I said.

"You have to promise to take me seriously."

"Yeah, of course. What is it?"

"No, really, Denny. You joke around a lot, but this is serious. It's weird, so don't be goofy about it, okay?"

"All right, I promise," I said, worrying it might be one of those questions a daughter asks her father—something that was going to make me uncomfortable.

"Sometimes I feel like I'm adopted," she said.

I smiled and lightly backhanded her shoulder. This was something I could address. "I understand, I really do," I said. "You suspect you're betraying the family."

A few tears slid down her quickly reddening cheeks.

"Want to know something funny? I've felt that way since I was about your age."

"And it's terrible," she said.

"You just have to be yourself, Mickey."

"It isn't right," she said.

"You know, it wouldn't surprise me if we weren't the only ones," I said. "Mom and Dad don't act like parents—not what I think of as parents, anyway."

She and I felt as if someone had dropped us into the wrong family. A feeling of detachment from them connected us.

After giving Mickey a tour of the UMSL campus, I had only one class to attend, Inorganic Chemistry—an introductory class, made difficult by its brilliant and demanding teacher, Dr. Charles Armbruster. Well studied in the sciences and the arts, Dr. Armbruster was an eloquent, handsome, Renaissance man.

We entered the upper level of a large classroom with stadium seating, and Mickey's eyes grew wide. "It's like a movie theater!" she said.

I left her standing near the doorway and then went down to talk to Dr. Armbruster, who was standing next to the podium at the base of the stage. He was six feet tall with neatly combed dark hair, and wore a sport coat, crisp shirt, and tie. Rumors surfaced weekly about the attractive women accompanying him to cultural events around town.

I motioned toward Mickey and asked Dr. Armbruster if she could sit in on the class. He strode up the aisle, weaving between arriving students, and headed straight toward Mickey, who looked as if caught in a nightmare attending class in her underwear. For a second, I thought she was going to run, but Dr. Armbruster offered his hand and with a broad, confident smile, he carefully leaned toward her as if she were made of delicate crystal. She extended her right hand while her left hand trembled as she tried to cover her mouth. When Mickey blushed, her face darkened like an overripe tomato, and the color stayed long past its biological purpose. She looked at me with a shrug that said, "Help?" Dr. Armbruster waved his open hand toward the empty seats, telling her to sit anywhere she'd like, and then he returned to his podium.

I sat several seats behind her, because I wanted her to get a sense of being a student like the rest of us. She kept glancing at me and waving me to sit with her.

"Stay there," I whispered, and watched her fall under Armbruster's captivating lecture on the synthesis of organometallic compounds.

During the drive home, we tossed around some possible majors Mickey could consider when she attended a university. Maybe the sciences, maybe the arts, but she was interested in how businesses worked, and thought an MBA might be her ticket.

Her awestruck reaction to a college professor—and not a movie star or a rock star—made me proud of her. She was excited, and when she was excited, her eyes seemed to turn from hazel to bright blue and reflect more of the world.

Topeka, Kansas, January 26, 1976: At 27, Tony is paroled from the Kansas State Reformatory, after serving the minimal five-year sentence. He is admitted to the Topeka VA Medical Center.

During six months of treatment, Tony is allowed to perform simple tasks as a volunteer aide. His EEG is abnormal and further indicates associated seizure disorder and familial hyperlipidemia interfering with his serum Dilantin level. On June 2, Tony is charged with theft of government property and sentenced to an additional six months, but he is released before the end of June. He stops taking his medications and begins using illegal drugs.

Marathon Key, Florida, August 20, 1976: Tony enters the home of Janette Wade, 25. He chokes her, repeatedly stabs her with a knife, and slits her throat. Hours later, Janette's husband, Stanley, comes home from work and finds the back door locked. He looks through the kitchen window and sees his two-year-old daughter, Jennifer, standing next to her mother who is lying dead in a pool of blood on the kitchen floor.

St. Petersburg, Florida, August 1976: Betty H. Brunton, a 52-year-old mother of four, walks home for lunch from her job at a nearby cemetery. Tony follows her into her home and stabs her to death with a bayonet he finds hanging on her wall.

Topeka, Kansas, July 1977: Tony marries his second wife, Janet Suther. A series of unsolved rape-murders begins to plague the state of Kansas. Several are in counties near Topeka.

Charlene and I separated in mid-1978. We'd tried counseling, but decided we had married before we had gotten to know each other well. She hated the Midwestern weather and was happy to fly back to California. I sank into an emotional funk for months until a woman at work invited me to attend a rock concert with her.

The group, Heart, was playing to a huge crowd in an auditorium a mile from my apartment. We sat in seats that were in the second from the last row—the thin oxygen section. It was like watching the musicians on C-SPAN, through their single stationary camera in the back of the auditorium. Afterwards, we went to my place, had a glass of white wine, and went to bed. Enjoying another woman's company was a kind of turning point, and I felt that I was ready to divorce Charlene.

I dropped by Mom's the next day, and Mickey came downstairs from her bedroom and plopped down next to me on the sofa. I thought she was tired, but she wasn't rubbing sleep from her eyes. She was having problems with another boyfriend, one who had proclaimed his love by writing her name on the city's highly visible water tower. This modern-day Romeo didn't want an exclusive relationship, and she did. I thought about a song I'd heard at the concert, so I took her to a record store and bought her Heart's new album, Dog and Butterfly.

The theme of the album's title song—handling rejection—is told through the wisdom an old man imparts to a woman who is having a hard time letting go of a relationship. The old man tells her about a dog chasing a butterfly. Every time the dog jumps for the butterfly and tries to catch it, the dog falls to the ground laughing and crying, ready to get back up and try again.

I thought the song's message was that finding and keeping love is a happy and sad adventure. We have some control over our own actions, but we shouldn't try to control someone we love. If Mickey's boyfriend truly wanted to be free, she would have to let him go, despite her hurt feelings. If he were as special as she had hoped he could be, he'd find his way back.

Mickey understood, and I felt I'd taught her a lesson about love that no one else in the family could have given her.

Topeka, Kansas, 1978: Tony is arrested for driving recklessly while having a seizure and is sentenced to one to ten years in the Kansas Department of Corrections. He is tested again at the Topeka VA Medical Center where his EEG shows numerous anomalies in the temporal and left hemisphere posterior regions. He is prescribed Dilantin for seizure disorder and encephalopathy. His jail sentence is suspended, and he is placed on five-years' probation. But he quickly breaks parole and receives another one- to ten-year sentence; however, he is released from the county jail by April.

St. Petersburg, Florida, May 20, 1978: Tony knocks Helen Alderson Hall, 60, to her bedroom floor and beats her with a lamp until she dies of multiple head wounds. The Halls are a prominent greyhound racing family.

Manhattan, Kansas, November 2, 1978: At approximately 10 a.m., two days before her 27th birthday, Tracey Miller returns home from a grocery store. Tony follows her into the house and rapes her. He stabs her in the chest 16 times and slits her throat. Three hours later, a neighbor discovers Tracey's 16-month-old daughter,

Emily, alone in the house with her mother's mutilated body.

Charlene had been phoning, writing, and sending me taped messages, trying to make a case for our getting back together. I felt our relationship was over, but she'd been working on Mom's sympathies.

"You might have changed your mind, but I still love my daughter-in-law," Mom said.

She offered to buy Charlene a round trip ticket and fly her to St. Louis for Christmas. I was suspicious about Mom's matchmaking attempts, but I finally gave in because she was so sincere in wishing to see things work out for us. After all, Charlene would have a prepaid ticket back to California.

But the return flight didn't happen, and Charlene stayed. Our daughter, Megan, was born on January 9, 1980.

Mickey called a few months later and asked if I would cosign a car loan with her. Mom had turned her down because Mickey had borrowed her ugly old AMC Gremlin one day and had driven it to school where someone had stolen it from the school parking lot. The question on everyone's mind was, "Who would steal a car that ugly?"

Mickey hadn't established credit anywhere, and the bank would not finance the car without the signature of someone with established credit.

I wanted to help her, but Charlene was more careful in handling our limited resources. With a new baby, we needed every penny. Summer was approaching, and we could afford only one small, used window air conditioner to cool all three rooms of our second-story flat. If it broke down, the heat and humidity would be almost unbearable for a newborn.

We had made it through the previous summer by taking frequent trips across the street and through the park to the art museum less than a mile away. St. Louis maintains a free public zoo and art museum by levying a small tax on people living or working within city limits. Charlene had become pregnant in April, and several times during the peak summer heat we had spent hours at the art museum, reading and looking at the collection of paintings and sculptures.

Mickey might also have contacted any of her other brothers or Joanie, or even Dad—I didn't ask. The point was that she had asked me, and I had good credit. Besides, some of our siblings couldn't get a loan for a go-cart.

As if turned out, a month after Mickey called, I wrecked my pea-green Ford Falcon while driving home alone from the UMSL campus, so Charlene and I would eventually need to finance a better car for ourselves. I'd been sitting at a red light for about ten seconds when I heard the sound of tires screeching. It was nearby, and I knew by the sound that the car had been traveling fast and that someone was going to be creamed. I glanced at my rearview mirror in time to see a car slam into the back of my car, which pushed it into the vehicle in front of me.

The shock of the impact drove me backward in my seat and wrenched my back, leaving me with a headache and muscle soreness for days. Someone once told me that green cars are the most likely to be rear-ended. They apparently register as grass to the unconscious minds of other drivers and become invisible, especially in suburbs or rural areas. White cars become almost invisible in snowfall, while brown cars blend in with the earth tones of fall. So my green car might as well have been shouting "Hit me!" to the traffic behind me. The car was still in working order, so I used the insurance money I'd received from the other driver to buy a new air conditioner for the apartment.

Topeka, Kansas, early July 1980: On his wedding anniversary, Tony finds Janet in bed with another man. He tries to kill her several times over the next two weeks, leaving town and returning after each attempt.

St. Charles, Missouri, mid-July 1980: Tony checks into a motel. Later, 43-year-old Patricia Modglin is found dead in her burning apartment nearby. She has been stabbed eleven times.

Police detectives Richard Plummer and Michael Harvey investigate a child molestation at Blanchette Public Park. The victim, a young boy, is traumatized, and his parents will not allow authorities to question him. The detectives know most of the local offenders and are suspicious that the perpetrator is from out of town.

One Saturday morning about a week after the car wreck, I was feeling better and stopped by Mom's house. Mickey had just returned from a week with a classmate at her family's summer home near Phoenix. The Arizona sun had lightened her hair and bronzed her skin.

We played the piano together before I left. She was beginning to lose interest in it, but Mom still kept it around. We tapped on several keys until we found the note corresponding to the nasal trumpet sound Dad used to make each time he'd blow his nose into one of his gray, wadded handkerchiefs—it was a G natural.

Years earlier, Mickey had shown me how to play one simple tune, "Heart and Soul." She had taught me how to play the rhythm and the melody, but I could never coordinate my hands to play both simultaneously. We each played one-handed and then switched sides on the keyboard. Every time I heard that song, it would remind me of the times we'd played it, laughing amid everyone's rising irritation. I never grew tired of it. We'd stop only after my fingers had grown weak and inaccurate, and even Mickey couldn't stand it any more.

Joanie happened to be at the house that day, and she yelled, "For Christ's sake, Mickey, teach him something else. You're driving us nuts!" spitting out the word *nuts* as if it contained an awful truth about our family.

Mom and Dad were always bickering over who was truly certifiable, each bringing more authentic-sounding jargon to the table as the exchange progressed.

"You're crazy, Joe. You're a lunatic!" she'd say.

"You're the goddamn crazy one," he'd answer.

"No. You're *really* crazy because you're too sick to know it. You're dangerous."

"You're paranoid," he'd say.

Mom would lower her voice and bring his family into the squabble.

"You're going to end up in the insane asylum, just like your brother. A certified manic depressive."

"Hey, I'll take a test any day," he'd answer.

"You couldn't pass an eighth-grade exam," she'd say. "What makes you think you could pass a test for mental stability? The Navy didn't even want you."

Mom's mother had deserted her when Mom was a child, and Dad knew right when to strike.

"Your own mother didn't want you. Goddamn crazy bitch," he'd say, usually ending the hate debate or escalating it to fisticuffs and flying ashtrays and kitchenware. We never knew which direction it would go, so we either laid low or left the house.

Mickey and I finished with the piano, and she followed me as far as the front porch.

I had parked my wrecked pea-grass-green Falcon across the street. The front bumper, bent downward from the impact of the crash, hung like an insect proboscis. Peeling paint exposed rust spots around the wheel wells, on fender creases and front headlights, and on folds in the metal where the rear section had been crushed. As I pried open the driver's door, the sound of metal grinding against metal broke the calm of the quiet morning.

Mickey burst into laughter, pointing at the heap. "How can you drive around in that thing? It's the ugliest car I've ever seen."

I used to love watching comedians do impersonations on television. I'd practice doing them myself in the bathroom mirror, and when I couldn't do an impression without laughing, I knew I had it down and I'd subject the family to it. I was always parading celebrities through the house: Ed Sullivan, Elvis, Mickey Mouse, Donald Duck, Porky Pig, Nixon, Jimmy Stewart, Edward G. Robinson, and (Joanie's favorite) the Hunchback of Notre Dame. Sometimes I'd combine them. I did a John Wayne who sounded like Richard Nixon.

Each time that our family moved—seven times during my grade school years—I became the new class clown. I had a good sense of comic timing, and I could tell a joke. Mike and Joanie were my biggest fans. She'd eventually reach critical mass and would beg me to stop before she wet her pants.

I never met a man who laughed so hard that he peed, but it's an issue with some women. In high school, I knew the *leakers*—and they'd run away when they saw me in the hallway between classes. "Please stop! Stop it," they'd beg. "I'm going to pee!" I loved to hear them plea. They might as well have been saying, "You're so talented and giving. You make me feel alive. I really like you." Mickey was a leaker.

Using humor as a way out of embarrassing situations came natural to me. So I pushed my shoulders up around my neck, adjusted an uncomfortable invisible necktie, and slammed the driver's door shut.

In my best Steve Martin, W*ild and Crazy Guy* voice, I said, "What, this car? Let me point out for you, if I may, beautiful lady, the many salient aspects of this unique vehicle." I walked back and forth alongside the car and pointed out defects as if they were attributes.

"First, you will notice the absence of hubcaps. We provide you with this benefit so that *you* will never have to replace them. They have been pre-stolen. These patches of brown are pre-rust features. They come standard with this package."

I pulled the driver's side door open again, sending a loud screech reverberating throughout the neighborhood.

Mickey stomped her feet and looked up and down the street, worried that a neighbor would come out and yell at me.

"We have equipped the door, as you may have noticed, with a unique theft alarm disguised as a very loud creak. Some thieves do not even realize when they set it off. Consider the urine green color. I notice that you are a teenager. Permit me to be frank, young lady. You will eventually be a designated driver for some of your drunken idiot friends. Okay, let's just call them drunks, but you will face this not right now, one or two of your drunks will probably throw up out the window. Well, this color will blend well with bile, and the creases catch and hide most of the chunks."

She held her stomach.

"Another safety feature, this is not a white car, so you will never lose it on a snowy winter day."

She jumped up and down on the porch.

"I see that you are concerned, Miss Prospective Car Buyer, with the rear end feature of this automobile.

She pressed her knees together and laughed hysterically.

"Stop it, Denny, please. I'm going to pee!"

I *had* her!

"This is our exclusive patented *pre-dent*, a feature available only on our low-end, urine-green, Ford Falcon vehicle-like conceptual cars. Miss Prospective Buyer, you are looking at the used car of the future worlds."

She stumbled, reached out, and grabbed the railing. I was laughing as hard as she was.

She ran into the house and I drove off, still smiling at the image of her standing on the porch laughing, covering her mouth with one hand, as if so out of control that she was about to spit up. I kept thinking about Mickey reaching for the porch railing, steadying herself with her other hand, bending at the knees, and squeezing her legs together, trying not to pee in her pants and embarrass herself—all the while looking at me with gratitude for the joy I'd given her.

I could make her laugh. I could always make her laugh.

St. Charles, Missouri, Monday, July 21, 1980: Tony visits Richard Roberson, a man with whom he had become acquainted during a recent trip to town. Roberson's home is located a few miles from 321 Glendale, the home of Mrs. Mildred A. Fleming (58). Mrs. Fleming lives with her two youngest daughters, Mary (nicknamed Mickey) (18), and Susie (19). Susie's one-year-old son also lives at the residence.

On Monday, July 21, 1980, I turned in my two-week notice at the small cosmetic and toiletry manufacturer where I worked as a quality control microbiologist. I had accepted a position and a thirty-percent pay raise with an independent drug-testing laboratory. Our daughter, Megan, was just over six months old, and the extra money made us more secure. Our marriage was going through another bump in the road, and we needed a positive change. I'd learned all I wanted to know about the science of hand lotions, shampoos, conditioners, and bubble baths. My new job testing pharmaceuticals would be far more interesting and a step up the career ladder. Life was about to get better, with fewer bills and a lot less stress.

That Wednesday afternoon, Charlene left Megan with a neighbor and met Mickey at the delicatessen where she worked part-time in the old town section of St. Charles. Mickey got off work early, and she and Charlene walked a block down the cobblestone street to an A&W root beer stand. They drank a couple of ice-cold mugs of root beer before driving out to Suntan Beach on the outskirts of the city. They sunbathed on the imported sand that lined the edge of the huge man-made lake and swam through the cool water out to the large dock floating like a giant raft at the lake's center. They made plans to return over the weekend, but didn't because that night Mickey was horsing around with a couple of her girlfriends and cracked the collarbone she had fractured when she was three.

321 Glendale, St. Charles, Missouri, Friday, July 25, 1980: Mildred Fleming leaves for work at 6:30 a.m. She exits through the back door and locks it.

One half hour later, Susie grabs her infant, leaves for work through the front door, and locks it. Mickey is asleep in her upstairs bedroom.

That Friday morning, July 25, I got up at 6 a.m., checked on Megan asleep in her crib, warmed up and stretched, and went across the street for a 3 mile run through Forest Park, a land mass greater than New York City's Central Park.

After a shower and breakfast with Charlene, I played a little with Megan and left the apartment at 7:30 a.m. I enjoyed the drive to work—20 minutes through city traffic—in the 1978 Toyota we'd purchased to replace the heap Mickey and I had laughed about just weeks before.

I got a cup of coffee from the lunchroom and said hello to my close friend, Tony, in the front offices, and then went to the chemistry lab to see if my boss, Norm, the chief chemist, had anything special for me.

Approximately 9 a.m. on July 25, Mickey is awakened by a phone call from her friend Elly

Sommerville. Mickey tells Elly she is nursing her collarbone and a migraine headache and is staying home from her summer job.

10:30 a.m. Claiming he needs the car for a job interview, Tony borrows Richard Roberson's yellow Buick convertible. He drives Richard to work, and then cruises a nearby neighborhood. He spots a 12-year-old girl riding a bicycle on Glendale Avenue and circles the block several times until the girl becomes frightened and pedals home.

He parks at a grocery store lot and then knocks on the door of a house across the street. A woman answers, and Tony asks for the time while wedging his foot in the door. When the woman's husband emerges from the kitchen, Tony politely leaves.

He returns to the car and is about to drive off when he sees Mickey Fleming approaching the store from the direction of her apartment. The teenager is wearing a bikini top and cut-off jeans with sandals.

She walks to the grocery store at the end of the block where she cashes a check and purchases some lettuce for a lunch salad she'd been preparing.

When she leaves the store, Tony follows her and enters the apartment through the back door.

Part II
Death and Mystery

Because I could not stop for Death,
He kindly stopped for me;
The carriage held but just ourselves
And Immortality. —Emily Dickinson

I gather samples from the day's production of shampoo, hand lotion, and bubble bath. My main responsibility is to test products for the presence of bacteria or molds, which indicates either lab contamination—something I did wrong—or process contamination—something that went wrong during manufacturing. Either way, it's a sign of something amiss, and my job is to hold back a product batch until I can confirm my lab test results.

It costs the company money to hold a batch, so if I make a mistake and get a false lab result, I waste company money. If confirmatory testing shows that the product is truly contaminated, the entire batch has to be discarded—this costs money too—but I'll look like a hero because releasing a contaminated product into the marketplace is not only a public safety issue, it can put a company out of business.

11 a.m. Mickey's friend Elly calls the apartment again. A stranger with a high-pitched voice answers. He giggles and sounds confused as if he's intoxicated. He tells Elly Mickey is not there and asks her to identify herself. Elly tells him her name, and the man promises to have Mickey call her back, and then hangs up. Elly redials and gets a busy signal.

11:05 a.m. A woman shopping at the grocery store, Ms. Rochelle Hord, sees Tony, dressed in white trousers and a buttoned down shirt, leave the front of the apartment and run to the yellow Buick convertible parked in the grocery store lot. As Tony speeds away, Ms. Hord notices the car has a loud muffler.

11:10 a.m. Wearing only her bikini top around her neck, Mickey runs naked out of the back of the apartment. Her forehead and right arm are bruised, and her fingers and hands are covered with numerous cuts. Blood spurts from several deep stab wounds in her chest, and her throat has been cut ear to ear nearly severing her head. She runs across the street to Robert and Dale Presser's front porch.

Robert Presser, 25, is home from his night shift at the railroad yards. He and his three-year-old daughter are watching cartoons in the front room. His wife, Dale, is ironing laundry near a bedroom window upstairs. Something outside catches her attention. She sees Mickey running from the rear of her apartment and directly toward the Pressers' front porch.

Dale screams and rushes downstairs to open the door, but Robert stops her and locks it. As Mickey desperately pounds on the door, Robert tells Dale to take their daughter upstairs and call 911. He grabs his shotgun and then runs out the back door and around to the front of the building.

Presser sees Mickey covered with blood, now collapsed on the concrete porch slab. He cautiously surveys the area. He calls to his wife to bring him a sheet, and then *covers the bleeding girl. Mickey tries to speak to him, but he cannot understand her.*

Tony drives over a small bridge a mile away, and tosses a stiletto knife with a broken tip into a muddy creek.

In my quality control lab, I review and record the results of microbiological tests in various stages of progress—some complete, others requiring an additional 24-72 hours of incubation. A test result on a baby shampoo sample shows bacterial growth and potential contamination, so I put the entire batch on hold until I can confirm the result—better to be safe than sorry.

11:15 a.m. An ambulance and several police cars arrive at the Pressers' apartment. A team of paramedics tries to save Mickey's life as a photographer snaps pictures. Police seal the apartment's exterior and doorways with yellow tape.

11:25 a.m. Mickey's brother, Brian, calls the Fleming residence to ask Mickey if they are going to go to Blanchette Park that afternoon. A police officer answers the phone and asks who is calling. Concerned, since Brian doesn't recognize the man's voice, he demands to know with whom he is speaking. The officer explains there's been an accident, and asks Brian where Mrs. Fleming can be contacted. Brian tells the cop Mrs. Fleming is at work at the Westinghouse Electric Company.

11:30 a.m. Westinghouse Electric Company, St. Charles: Mrs. Mildred Fleming receives a phone call at work. She is urged to have someone drive her to the emergency room at St. Joseph's Hospital.

I'm in the processing section of the plant, where 5,000–10,000-gallon batch tanks feed nine lotion and shampoo production lines, amid dozens of employees trying to talk over the racket of machines capping and labeling bottles. As I'm placing a red restraining sticker on a holding tank of baby shampoo, I become aware of the intercom blaring, "Dennis Fleming, pick up line two. Dennis, pick up line two." The decades-old speakers make the receptionist sound as if she's pinching her nose.

I grab a phone on a thick, wood support column fifty feet away. A strange yet familiar voice comes through static, like an overseas connection. It's Mom.

"I can't hear you, Mom. You sound like you're far away," I say. I see her in my mind as tiny or shouting at me from a distance. She is saying something about Mickey.

"Mickey what?" I ask. She repeats something about Mickey, but it makes no sense. I jiggle the line connected to the phone, but it doesn't help. "What's wrong, Mom? Can you speak up?"

"Mickey is dead, Denny! She's dead."

"Bullshit," I say. "What's really wrong?" I know that something probably *is* wrong, but Mom dramatizes things—and I hate to pry information from her.

"I'm telling you, Denny, Mickey's dead! Somebody murdered her."

That doesn't make sense. Murder? Mickey dead? It's *crazy*.

"No. What happened?" I ask. "Was she in a car accident?"

Suddenly, Mom doesn't seem far away or tiny. Her thin, soft voice is clear now. She simply doesn't have the strength to be louder. She's been speaking with as much effort as she can manage, which isn't much.

"She was stabbed to death in the house," she says. "You have to come to the hospital right away."

"Stop it! Why are you saying all this?"

"I had to identify the body. I'm at the hospital in St. Charles."

I finally accept the truth.

"Do they know what happened?"

She tries to say more, but I can't make it out.

"You're not telling me this, Mom. Tell me this isn't happening."

"Come to the hospital, Dennis. Your little sister is dead."

Pressure begins building in my chest and tightening my throat. Mom needs some form of corroboration that the horrible situation she is facing is real.

"I'm on my way. I'll be there as fast as I can," I say, fumbling the receiver and twisting the cord in knots before slamming it down. I'm nauseated as if I've been gut-punched and slapped hard in the back of the head.

Wait, what is it I have to do? I just told someone I would do something, but I stand motionless, staring at the wood column in front of me. The thick grain seems frozen in a slide toward the floor. If I can just stand here and look at it long enough, my world will go back to the way it was. I have to leave, *but why*?

I'm breathing fast, at the top of my chest, and pain is spreading from above my heart to my shoulders and neck. My thoughts crystallize. I remember why I have to leave, so I start walking toward my boss's office, but then I stop. *What am I doing, again?*

Someone behind me says, "That didn't sound like a good phone call. What's going on?"

I turn around, but I can't make out the person's face hidden by shadows cast by several high-stacked pallets of boxes.

"That was my mother," I say. "She called from the hospital. My little sister is dead." I turn away and pretend to check a release sticker on a stack of pallets loaded with cases of hand lotion. I wipe the tears from my cheeks with the sleeve of my white lab coat. The faceless person in the shadows mumbles something that I don't understand.

I enter Norm's office and try to speak, but I can't get anything out. He asks me what's wrong and motions to a chair, but I find myself standing, sobbing, and facing an empty corner behind the shelves in the sample room *behind* Norm's office.

"My sister is dead. I have to leave and go to the hospital," I say, wondering if I've been standing here for thirty seconds or five minutes. It is very quiet.

On my way out of Norm's office, I hear distant voices of people talking to me and trying to console me—but I can't grasp what they're saying. My friend Tony grabs my arm and leads me toward the front door. Pat Farrell, a lab technician I see nearly every day, stops us.

A few weeks ago, Pat told me what it meant to lose her brother. It bothered her to talk about it, and I felt privileged that she confided in me. I *thought* I understood the pain she must have felt. But now some force is pulling away a giant piece from the top of my heart, and my whole body is screaming into a vast nothingness it's leaving behind.

Pat throws her arms around me, but I experience no sensation of being hugged. She whispers in my ear, her voice sincere and certain. "You will get through this," she says. Her words are strong, and for a moment, I believe her.

Police officers and detectives dust the Fleming residence for fingerprints and search for evidence. They find a pair of cutoff jeans and sandals on the front living room floor. They take blood and hair samples from the walls, end tables, coffee table, and a large puddle of blood in the middle of the floor. An open and blood-splattered purse containing over a hundred dollars rests in the center of the coffee table.

They follow a long red smear from the living room through the hallway and into the kitchen. My sister's panties, spotted with blood, lie on the kitchen floor. Several eggs are still cooking in a pot of boiling water on the kitchen stove. A partially prepared green salad is on the counter.

The back door is streaked with blood. The police track splatters and footprints of it across the back porch in the direction of the Pressers' across the street.

The drive to the hospital in St. Charles takes about twenty-five minutes. The sun is high overhead amid a sky of drifting white clouds. Everything seems too bright. Warm air rushes through the open windows, and the day seems to be the opposite of what it should be. Missourians usually suffer in the July humidity, but today is dry and beautiful.

Tony and I have been friends since I started with the company two years ago. We share a common love of intellectual pursuits—literature, politics, and art. I'm grateful he volunteered to drive. I can't.

He keeps wiping his tears as he tries to calm me. His steadiness makes me realize how much I'm out of control. I try to talk, try to understand what's happening; I bend forward, scream and cry uncontrollably, and then the cycle repeats itself. An invisible force is pulling on my chest and trying to rip out a part of my heart. The physical pain is real. A heart attack doesn't enter my mind.

St. Joseph's Hospital sits on a hillside overlooking the Missouri River three blocks to the east. Tony drops me off at the emergency room entrance. He sits tightly gripping the steering wheel with both hands, searching for the right words.

"You need to do this with your family, Dennis."

We see Mark and Brian standing near the emergency room door. They're smoking cigarettes and glancing toward the river or down at the sidewalk in front of them.

"Call me if there is anything I can do," Tony says, as he pulls away from the curb. I hurry toward my brothers and go straight to Mark—the calm, quiet one. His face, normally red from the summer sun, has lost its color.

"Is it true? Is Mickey really dead?" I ask. Before Mark can say anything, Brian interjects. He never grew out of his childhood habit of pushing his way into conversations. As the youngest brother, he always finds it necessary to show he stands on equal ground with the rest of us.

"We've got to find the son of a bitch before the cops find him, brother Denny!" he says, throwing his cigarette down and toe-twisting it into the sidewalk. "Then we gotta kill the motherfucker." *Am I prepared to do that?* I wonder.

I find Mom in the ER waiting room sitting near a phone behind a small counter, which seems appropriate, since it feels as if she just called me two minutes ago. *How many calls similar to mine has she made?* Her face is pale and streaked from crying.

I hug her, but I'm angry with her. She always gets things confused when she's upset and then gets everyone in a panic. She lights a fresh cigarette from another she's still smoking. I take one from the pack and light it with a lighter lying next to the full ashtray in front of her.

"Are you absolutely sure about all this, Mom?" I ask, holding onto the possibility that maybe Mickey is only badly hurt—*but dead?* It just seems impossible. Mom always makes things seem worse than they are.

"Mom?"

She covers her face with her hands and begins to cry.

"I had to identify her body, Denny. Her throat was cut…and they stabbed her."

A nurse in her thirties walks up, places her hand on Mom's shoulder, and rubs in circles below the base of her neck. Even as a professional, she's far too calm for someone involved in the murder of an innocent teenage girl. I ask the nurse if she's *positive* Mickey's dead.

"Yes, I'm afraid so, sir," she says softly, showing no emotion. *How can she be so autocratic, so unaffected? Why isn't she as upset as we are?*

She pulls a chair toward me.

"You have seen her, seen the body?" I ask.

"I'm really sorry, Mr. Fleming. Would you like to sit down? Can I get something for you?"

Mom stands, and for the first time she shows some strength.

"His name is *Dennis*," she says, and grabs a tissue from a dispenser on the counter before slumping back into her chair.

"I want to see her," I say. "Can I see her?"

A middle-aged nurse approaches us.

"Dennis, my name is Beth. I can get you something to calm you down."

"I don't need anything to calm me down! I *just* want to see my sister! I *just* want to look at her, that's all."

There's a time lapse between the words I yell and the realization that they are coming from my mouth. Each passing second feels like an hour.

Beth crosses the room and tries to calm Mark and Brian, who are inside now and talking over each other's sentences.

The younger nurse says she'll ask the attending physician if I can see Mickey's body. To no one in particular I scream, "I'm okay, damn it! I don't need anything. I just want to see my sister. I have a right to see my own sister."

A man with a serious demeanor and dressed in blue scrubs comes through a set of double doors. I think I see a trace of sympathy cross his otherwise stoic face.

"I understand that you want to view the body, Mr. Fleming," he says matter-of-factly, "but I closed the examination, and since this is a case under investigation, we would have to get legal authorization to reopen it."

"Then get it! I have to see her! I have to see her dead body."

"I know that hearing what I just told you is difficult, and that you're having trouble accepting this traumatic event, Mr. Fleming, but your mother has already identified the body."

"I know. She told me. But I still want to see her!"

"Look, Mr. Fleming," the doctor says, the tone of his voice softening, "your sister played on my daughter's softball team. I knew Mary, she was strong, and there was only a small chance that we could save her. I opened her chest, but the heart had been damaged." The way the doctor said *the heart* sounded cold and clinical.

"*Her* heart," I say. "*Her* heart. She's a person!" Everyone at the hospital is treating us so cordially, so calmly. *Can't they see what this is doing to me—to all of us?*

"I'm very sorry for you and your family. Please try to understand—this isn't something that a loved one should see. As I said, I'd have to follow several legal steps to reopen the examination, and you really don't need that memory. It will be far better if you remember Mary as she was."

"She graduated early," I say, and the pride of that statement slips away into emptiness as quickly as I form the words. Why did I say that? She hadn't started or finished school early, but why did that come out? I always get her date of birth wrong.

In my head, I know he's right. It makes no sense to see Mickey's bloody, abused body—but I still can't believe she's dead, and no amount of third-person testimony makes it seem real. Mickey's only eighteen. She just graduated from high school and is going to college. People who live through traumatic situations say it all seem surreal. I know exactly what they mean. Part of me knows I'm in denial.

My older sister, Joanie, and her husband, Bob, arrive. Joanie always gets the family news before I do, and I know she is going to act as if she hasn't heard anything about Mickey's murder. But she has to know. She walks straight to me and leans slightly forward as if to hear a secret I have for her.

"What is going on?" she asks, and slightly raises her eyebrows. I hate the way we act uninformed so we can draw the spotlight. Someone had to have called Joanie, or she wouldn't be here. She knows exactly what's going on. I lock eyes with her and point to the double doors the doctor had just come through.

"Mickey's in there," I snap. "She's dead. Somebody cut her up. That's what's going on—and you Goddamn well know it!"

Joanie reaches for Bob and steadies herself. *Does she really not know or is she in denial, too?* She regains her composure.

"Damn you, Denny! Bob called me at work and then picked me up. He told me we were going to the hospital right away. That's all! You'd better be lying, damn it!"

Joanie looks at Mom and instantly knows I'm not lying. I hug her.

"I'm sorry," I say. She feels like stone.

The doctor who spoke to me takes her aside, and the two begin speaking in hushed tones. Joanie screams. She has awakened. The nightmare is really happening.

I go outside, walk down to the river, and sit on a wooden bench. It would be foolish to pray. After all, why would God grant me anything special? I'm an agnostic, but I prayed in the past—for peace or for someone else. I think of God as a non-associated deity, undefined, and not restricted to any particular religion. I always capitalize the noun when writing, which personalizes it in a way. I always hope my prayers will be answered, but I never expect a direct response.

Maybe I've never been humble—truly humble. The truth is I don't know if I can be humble. It requires a modesty I don't possess. I pray anyway—I pray with honesty, a deep sincerity I've never felt or expressed before. It's authentic. I'm prepared to believe anything, to do anything for Mickey, so I pray.

"Dear God. What can I say to you? Am I a fool for coming to you now? I have to beg. I'm going to ask you for something that's not just for me—it's for my whole family. Please give Mickey back to us. Heal her and give her back."

I slide off the bench and kneel in the dirt. "I don't think anyone knows exactly how you do things. Maybe you plan things, maybe you don't. Maybe what seems random is part of your intention, or maybe you control everything, every detail. I'm asking you now, please change this situation. You can take me instead of Mickey. I've lived longer, and I know I should pay for some things I've done, but Mickey doesn't deserve to die this young, and in this way."

Life and death and God. What's the point? I have some idea of what life is all about—about the big picture —but I don't know anything. My little sister is gone, lying dead on a slab in a cold examination room. Only hours before, she was alive, and I was at work, and everything was fine—but nothing will ever be the same again.

It will all change me somehow, in some way—I'm certain it will. It will change all of us.

There's no sense to it, no way of looking at Mickey's death that puts it into perspective. It's like a bomb tossed into a daycare center. What could have caused *this*? Did she smart off to some scumbag who decided to pay her back? She couldn't have brought it upon herself.

I'm cold, yet I'm sweating, struck with the horror that someone meant to kill her and then killed her in this terrible way. A car accident would at least make sense—that's what I thought at first—or an overdose while experimenting with drugs. Even a suicide, in *some* way would give me something to grasp onto, but Mickey had no choice in this—it wasn't an accident.

Someone could have chosen not to do it—but did it anyway.

1:10 p.m. Dressed in a T-shirt and cutoff jeans, Tony picks up Roberson from work, and they have lunch at his house. They laugh and joke around, and Tony offers to paint Roberson's car as a way to show his appreciation for letting him stay while he job hunts.

The Missouri River seems muddier, wider, and faster than usual. The sky has grown gray, and threatens to rain. I make my mind up not to test God. If he hears me and chooses to save Mickey's life, someone will tell me—no doubt about that.

Later that afternoon, I find myself talking to detectives, deputies, and other members of the Major Case Squad, an emergency team that assembles for major crimes like murder and high-profile kidnappings and rapes. Twenty-five professionals are working continually on the case, ten officers from St. Charles, and fifteen from nearby counties such as St. Louis.

I'm in a blackout from the afternoon to the evening. I lose a critical period of my life, but at least I have a life.

I don't remember anything specific about the night either, except that I talk to the police and volunteer to help them run down leads. They send my brothers on various missions too, designed to help solve the case—and to keep five enraged men busy over the next several days.

The police pair me with my brother-in-law, Bob, because he is relatively calm and rational. I receive an assignment, and then I meet with squad members and tell them what I discovered, and they give me a new assignment. Bob drives around patiently, providing me with a steady diet of cigarettes, coffee, beer, and an occasional shot of whiskey. When we're offered pot somewhere, I grab that too. It's a nightmare, like living scenes from a long-forgotten piece of film noir. My mind doesn't attach to much of anything, beyond riding with Bob in his car, driving in endless circles.

Late at night, we stop several times for coffee or cigarettes at a Quick Stop gas station. I step out into the milky white or yellow glow of their three a.m. neon lights, and I seem trapped in another dimension. It's as if I'm standing at the very top of the Earth, bathed in a hellish incandescent light, where nothing else exists in the darkness beyond its boundaries. I know that we will eventually leave, travel around, and then stop somewhere else, and I'll return to that strange light once more—in a surreal cycle that will never end.

During one of several stops at Bob and Joanie's, I'm standing on their manicured front lawn when a detective in a sport coat and a gun on his hip takes me aside. He's excited because he has a lead.

"I've talked to a lot of people tonight and one thing I know for sure," he says. He puts his hand on my shoulder the way a father comforts his son after the boy's team lost a football game. "Your sister was about as straight an arrow as you can find. I think I'm going to get this bastard, and I'm praying that the son of a bitch runs. It'll save a lot of bullshit and taxpayer money. If they take him in, the scum will probably get off light somehow."

It seems fitting for me to feel that way about Mickey's murderer, but cops aren't supposed to think like vigilantes. Professionals aren't supposed to talk this way. I understand his anger, but he isn't the one who is living with a piece of his heart missing. If anyone does away with this animal, it should be one of us, and I want it to be *me*. Whether this cop catches the killer or not, I won't complain—as long as we get him.

The next day, one of the detectives asks me if Susie is up to taking them through the apartment. Mom's a wreck and has already said she'll never enter the building again. Since Susie and her one-year-old son— who is now safe with his other grandmother—share the apartment, she might be able to spot something out of the ordinary, something the police might miss.

I call Susie expecting her to decline. She hasn't slept in forty-eight hours. Our brothers, Mike and Kevin, flew in from California, and everyone has been drinking heavily. She is eager to help the police and meets me and several detectives an hour later at the apartment.

Two detectives escort us toward the yellow perimeter tape around the apartment. A reporter with a clipboard cautiously approaches and asks if he can have a word with me. I look at one of the detectives for guidance, and he says he can't tell me not to talk to the press, but that this might not be a good time, so I blow the reporter off.

Susie, pale and fragile, walks through the place, room by room, as if trapped in a dream. I drag myself along. Maybe I'll see something.

Susie shows no reaction to the thick red streaks on the kitchen walls or the trail of blood that leads to the dark purple spot, the size of an open manhole, on the living room carpet.

The shag fibers lie flat from the weight of Mickey's blood pressing them lower than the rest of the carpet. He pinned her there while she struggled, losing a lot of blood, before he dragged her into the kitchen to rape her.

Susie escorts the detectives upstairs while I stay in the living room. Squatting near the carpet stain, I want to see something—some residual evil, perhaps. I hope that I can somehow see an instant of it—maybe a face, like the ghostly afterimage a camera flash leaves on my eye.

"Let me see his face," I pray silently. "Please let me see his face—or where he is right now. We need to stop him before he does this again. Just his face will be enough." I look around the room, hoping for a vision, frightened that I actually will receive one. A familiar emptiness fills me as it had yesterday by the river.

I rise to join the others upstairs, but stop beside Mickey's piano at the base of the stairway. There is no blood, but the wooden sheet music stand above the keyboard is broken. It is splintered, and a brass screw on its base is bent and pushing the wood apart. Did he knock Mickey into it? It might be a byproduct of family horseplay—but maybe not. Did the killer throw her into the piano just inches away from where Mickey and I laughed and tapped the keys so often?

Then, it occurs to me that she must have screamed during the struggle. I hadn't thought of that, hadn't let myself imagine it. Did she cry out for one of her brothers? Did she cry out for Mike or Mark or Kevin or Brian? Did she cry out for me? The question will haunt me. Did Mickey cry out for me? Was I in her mind during those final moments?

I point out the piano damage to Susie and the detectives when they come back downstairs. As far as she knows, the music stand on the piano was intact when she left the house yesterday morning, or at least, she's unaware if it had been broken.

On the way out, Susie tells me Mickey's friend Elly called the apartment and Mickey told her she had a headache and was staying home, but when Elly called to see if Mickey would go to lunch, a man who laughed nervously and sounded like he was drunk answered. He hung up, and Elly called back but the line was busy.

Mom later confirms that the piano was probably damaged during the struggle.

It brings the ugliness of Mickey's death even closer to me.

Topeka, Kansas, July 27, 1980: Roberson drives Tony to Topeka from St. Charles and drops him off at his sister's apartment. Tony tells Roberson to let him know if he runs into any trouble back in St. Charles because he will take care of it. Roberson thinks the comment is odd.

Suspicion and confusion infect my every thought during the manhunt for Mickey's murderer. Everyone connected to our family is a suspect, from Mom's boyfriend of five years to the young man who dated Mickey for the first time the night before. The brutal way she died, the attempted rape, and the deep stabbing and slicing are all signs that the killer is a man.

I can't help any of Mickey's male friends grieve. I can't allow myself to get close emotionally to any of them. They are all suspects. I have to pull away, and I'm filled with guilt over it. They are her friends, they are pouring out their grief and sympathies to me, and it pains me to stand at a distance.

Mickey's wake and funeral are nightmares. Trembling, wailing teenagers, held upright by stronger companions, drag their feet into the funeral parlor and past the open casket. Many are close friends from her graduating class. She's a popular student and plays on the school's softball and basketball teams. The horrific nature of the killing has upset them all, and they haven't slept well over the weekend.

Until now, the worst thing most of them have experienced is their parents' divorce or a friend injured in a car accident. They're not prepared to see Mickey lying in an open casket.

At funerals, mourners often say, May she rest in peace. But she doesn't appear to be at rest, as if the terror of her last moments refuse to remain hidden beneath the mortician's makeup. To conceal the deep ear-to-ear knife wound, they pulled her chin toward her throat, which makes her look heavier.

I want to look at her for a long time. She's wearing her new green dress, the one she told her friend Martha "...makes me feel beautiful." I don't want to believe I will never see her again. But she doesn't look like Mickey, so I turn away.

I want to believe in something beyond physical life—a place where Mickey can be happy. I want to believe Mickey's last moments of consciousness released her from the horror of her death, but I can't find comfort in the empty shell of her body.

I've been without food and sleep for almost seventy-two hours, yet I manage to push myself through the ordeal and the funeral, trying to look strong for my family. I am literally empty inside—one of the walking dead.

Every time I drop into a chair, I brush against one of the huge flower arrangements that fill the funeral parlor. Mickey's friends went overboard with large ornate cards and loads of flowers. My heart tries to go out to these horrified teenagers, but I'm hollow and useless. Their tears and their obvious respect for my little sister comfort me mentally—my emotions won't allow any comfort. I can't do anything for them.

The thought that Mickey would be the first to leave us has never entered my mind. Why would it? She is the youngest, plays sports, and is averse to cigarettes, alcohol, and drugs. She is the healthiest and the most fit, the gem of our family.

We are all broken in some way from growing up in the chaos of our household, but Mickey emerged intact —and for what?

The murderer breaks a part of me, a part that is physically connected to my heart—he invaded a part that only Mickey and I share. The killer tore something out of me—my soul?—and the only thing that rushes in to fill that hole is hate.

I want to find the man who did this to Mickey. I want someone to lock me in a room with him so I can kill him barehanded. Shooting him, or stabbing and slicing him up the way he butchered her, isn't enough. I want to beat him, to strangle him, and to dig my nails into the soft tissue of his abdomen. I want to reach under his ribs and rip out his heart while it's still beating. Then I want to bite into it, spit a piece of it into his face, and watch him die.

In the Marine Corps, they trained me to kill, trained me to puncture eyeballs and extract them, trained me to knock out the enemy and then to dispense with him any way I wanted. I never unleashed those skills, but a raw, violent hatred seizes me and gives me the perfect reason for putting my training to use. The incomprehensibility of the murder fills me with rage and hate so intense that it's swallowing me and tainting my every emotion.

One of Mom's friends, who knows that Mom named Mickey after the mother of Jesus, brings a small, green plant—it looks like a lily of some type—in a ceramic Madonna "Virgin Mary" planter. It's a simple thing, a cream-colored, eight-inch bust of Mary with her hands folded in prayer, her head tilted slightly to the right. But the four-inch, thin-leaved plant, though comparatively small, stands out among all the oversized flower arrangements with their giant ribbons and large cards. The planter's a tacky assembly line ceramic, but it has an aesthetic quality that I appreciate.

I tell Mom it reminds me of the sculpture, *Mademoiselle Pogany*, by Constantin Brancusi.

I saw a *Mlle. Pogany* series at the St. Louis Art Museum. The early stages resemble a woman in prayer, like the Virgin planter, but his later pieces are abstracts, as are most of Brancusi's works. The exhibit inspired me to attempt to turn a large oak stump into a mother-and-child sculpture. Oak is an extremely hard wood and probably the last choice for carving. I tore into the wood with a hatchet and hammers, and I ruined several good screwdrivers. I grew frustrated and finally gave up, but the experience initiated in me an interest in sculpture.

Before we carry the casket out of the building, we watch Mom grow hysterical in the funeral parlor during her last moments with Mickey's body. She grabs the handles on the side of the casket and begins screaming and rocking it. Two parlor attendants can't pull her away, so I step out of the crowd and move toward her, but a powerful hand brushes me aside.

"I'll get her," Dad says, pulling the attendants out of the way.

He tugs Mom so hard that I think the casket is going to crash to the floor. She stumbles back, and Dad holds onto her, both of them nearly fall. They embrace and console each other by their dead daughter. It's been many years since I've seen any real tenderness between them. They've been divorced for a decade, during which Dad has been nothing but contemptible and mean-spirited toward Mom, yet at this moment, he is the only one who can comfort her.

St. Charles, Missouri, July 29, 1980: News articles link Roberson's convertible to the killing. Roberson calls Tony in Topeka. The killer is reluctant to talk about the murder.

An employee at a St. Charles paint shop questions why he had been contacted to paint a car fitting the description of a car identified at a murder scene. He calls police.

Law enforcement officials contact Roberson who calls Tony again. This time, a police officer listens in as Tony tells Roberson he doesn't know why he killed the girl. Then he says she started yelling and tried to run. He says he plans to stay away from his parents' home for thirty days until the heat is off.

At the gravesite, I'm lost among a crowd of friends and strangers sobbing, patting me, or throwing their arms around me. *Was I a pallbearer? How did I get to the cemetery?* I'm numb and disconnected, and I can't identify with the sadness swirling all around me. I work hard to come up with something about the way she died that wasn't sickening.

At least her suffering wasn't prolonged. It could have been far worse. If Mickey hadn't run out of the apartment, Mom, or Susie, or Susie's toddler would have found the mutilated body. Thank God she ran.

Police officers I recognize from the investigative whirlwind of the last three days are mingling about in plain clothes. One tells me they're observing the crowd and watching the cemetery periphery. He says perpetrators of such crimes sometimes watch the burial of their victims as part of their ritual. Some of Mickey's high school friends have brought their parents along for support—and every face I don't recognize becomes a suspect in my mind.

The night before the murder, Mickey had gone on a first date with a twenty-year-old man named John. Some Major Case Squad cops went to his place of employment shortly after the murder. They took John to the station for an extended interrogation.

John had led the police to his apartment, where he voluntarily showed them his extensive collection of knives and primitive weaponry, which he openly displayed on the walls. They had spent hours each day since the murder trying to get him to break down.

He is understandably anxious about Mickey's five brothers, all of us brought up in construction work, who might find a reason to go after him. We've all degenerated to Dad's behavior, knocking back shots of whiskey and beer to try to drown our pain. Cocked and ready to fire, any one of us will go off if we think we've found the animal who killed our baby sister.

Sweating and looking scared through bloodshot eyes, John approaches me at the cemetery. He pleads with me to believe he had nothing to do with Mickey's death, but I can't honestly tell him that I believe him. He is skinny, smokes cigarettes, and wears a mustache. He doesn't seem like Mickey's type at all. His date with her the night before the murder would probably have been their last. It isn't too hard to imagine Mickey turning down his advances that night. Maybe he is mentally unstable, and returned the next day, and killed her in a rage.

The gray casket hangs above its rectangular hole in the ground, and I'm helpless, pathetic, and inadequate. I've been thoughtless, and haven't prepared any last remembrance to send Mickey into eternity. Isn't there some way that I can honor my dead sister better than just letting them shove her into the ground?

Someone had carefully arranged a bouquet of red roses at the side of the grave, and I decide to place a single rose on the casket as a symbolic gesture of my love for her. However, the roses are tied together with wire, so I twist and pull on a single flower, trying to untangle it as the casket begins descending.

Running out of time, I rip one rose from the bunch, but a thick piece of wire, bent like a fishing hook, tears into my finger. I yank the wire out, and my finger starts bleeding freely. I reach across the rounded top of the casket and release the rose, but it begins sliding off, so I quickly adjust its position until it stays put.

When I withdraw my hand, I see what a mess I've made by smearing the top of the casket with blood. I'm embarrassed. My gesture of love, a single flower, meant to symbolize that my heart will always be with Mickey, has come across as melodramatic—a delicate rose, ripped in blood and anger from its family—a cheap cliché. Instead of honoring Mickey, I've drawn attention to myself through this botched gesture. *Oh, look at Denny and his symbolic blood rose of love.* I hate myself.

My knees buckle. I tremble and turn away from the grave. It feels like I'm carrying the weight of the casket on my back, and I want to lie down. My next-door neighbor, Anne, and her best friend, Patricia, take turns holding me upright, but all I can think about is keeping my hand high to avoid dripping blood onto their white blouses.

Others are throwing handfuls of dirt on the casket. I look around for Mom. She's sitting in the front passenger side of a car parked fifty feet away at the cemetery's edge. She's left the door wide open. How'd she get there so fast? Is she unable to watch them lower her youngest child into the ground? I'll be strong, for her sake. I'm the college boy, the smart one, the ex-Marine. My mother needs some way to believe that things will be okay.

Pale and motionless, staring at the dashboard, she's in shock or deep in prayer. I kneel beside her.

"It's terrible, Denny," she says. "We don't deserve this."

I start to put my arm around her small, rounded shoulders and tell her that no one deserves such a tragedy, and that we'll get through it—but the idea seems absurd. Our family can't scarcely get through a barbecue.

Instead, I burst into tears and babble like a baby. "Who killed my little sister, Mommy? Who took Mickey away from me?"

I put my head in her lap, and we cry together. She strokes my hair the way she did when I was five.

I think about what Mom said: "We don't deserve this." Does she think Mickey's death is punishment for our family's sins? Mom has a profound sense of Catholic guilt. She can transform the entire horrible event into something that is *our* fault. I had similar thoughts at the gravesite, and I'm an agnostic. How can anyone who loves another so much be blamed for anything so horrible? It's insane thinking.

I suddenly realize that no one can blame me for losing control at the grave. Nothing I can do to attempt to honor my sister could dishonor her.

I'm *glad I bled* on Mickey's coffin, and it seems entirely fitting that she's taking part of me with her into the ground.

Topeka, Kansas: Tony searches for his wife, Janet, at his sister's and at his parents'. At one point, he hallucinates and believes he has murdered Janet.

Detectives Plummer and Harvey are dispatched to Kansas to track down suspect Anthony J. LaRette Jr. They stake out LaRette's apartment, his parents' home, and his sister's home.

That night, we move Megan's crib into our bedroom. It gives us a sense of comfort having our precious new daughter close to us. While lying exhausted in my bed, I look at Megan lying peacefully in her crib, a mobile of colorful, fluffy animals hanging motionless above, like pets patiently waiting for their next go around. Charlene lies beside me, holding my hand, trying to relax. The random, senseless, and violent nature of Mickey's murder is shaking her, too.

I control my breathing, four counts inhaling, eight counts exhaling, trying to calm myself and quiet my heart, which, as a runner, I monitor regularly. It's beating a rapid 130 beats per minute, my running pace.

The window air conditioner labors to keep the three-room apartment cool, but the air is clammy. I think about how proud I'd been at Megan's birth and how much joy she'd brought into our lives. An idea floated around in my head at the funeral. Perhaps we should give Megan the nickname Mickey. But I realize I would confuse emotions between my sister and my daughter. I won't subject my daughter to that. "No way!" I think.

"Life is strange," I say softly. "One life ends, another begins."

"Megan has an angel to watch over her now," says Charlene, and she gently squeezes my hand. "Her Aunt Mickey."

The animals above Megan's bed begin to rotate, and the mechanism plays a few notes of its tune. The room begins to glow. I become aware of Mickey's spirit everywhere in the room—a tangible cool breeze that passes through me.

"Do you feel that? Can you see the white glow?" I ask.

"I felt *something*," Charlene whispers, as if she doesn't want to wake Megan and alert her to whatever has just entered the room.

My scientific mind wants to explain how such a thing can happen. For instance, Megan's mobile has a windup mechanism that might have been jarred when we moved the crib into our bedroom, but what has just activated it? Megan might have caused a vibration in the mechanism when she rolled over in her sleep, though the room has been quiet, and we haven't heard any movement. Perhaps our senses manufactured the glow by extrapolating a spiritual event from a random noise and a fear of the unknown. There has to be a rational explanation, but we decide to take comfort in an understanding that Mickey is telling us that, yes, she is going to watch over Megan.

However, feeling that Mickey still exists in some form doesn't comfort me for long. The urge to kill a man grows strong in me. I worry that a Major Case Squad officer, or one of my brothers, will get to him first and take away my opportunity. I not only hate the killer, I'm obligated to hate him. Somehow, not hating him challenges my character.

How can I *not* hate him and still respect myself? The storm's been following me everywhere, and I have to deal with it again and again. Every day I weaken further, so I choose to own the emotion—let it bear down on me like the pressure at the bottom of the deep end of a swimming pool. I snap at Charlene over little things. I hit walls, and scream when Megan won't stop crying. I pull doors closed on my hand, lock myself out of my car, and run stop signs. I'm out of breath after running a mile.

I'm not myself, and I'm beginning to wonder who is the real me? If, by some miracle, I do manage to be in a room with the killer, do I have what it takes to do what I'm telling myself and everybody else I will do, kill him with my bare hands? I keep praying for the chance, but can I do it?

I have two choices—live with the struggle or subdue it. It's becoming a part of me, taking precedence over my emotions: joy, fear, disgust, and sorrow. Even worse, it's interfering with my feelings for Mickey. I can't think of her without feeling immense hatred for the man who showed her the very worst in what a man can be before taking her life. Loss and hatred are pulling me apart, and I want to destroy the cause of the pain. I'm becoming angrier and less loving every day.

I have to replace this loathing with something. But with what? For days, I can't come up with anything.

So I choose to disown it, and in doing so, refuse to let it be a part of me any more. I find its replacement. I will honor Mickey by creating something positive from her brutal death—by doing more with *my* life. That way, in some way, her death will make the world better through me.

Dad offers a ⊠5,000 reward for information leading to the capture of Mickey's killer. He planned to use the money to buy her a car, the one I couldn't afford to help her finance.

I'm keeping myself busy visiting the family, Joanie in St. Louis County, Dad in the City of St. Louis, Susie and my brothers at Mark's apartment in St. Charles.

On my way to Mark's, I'm driving by St. Joseph's Hospital when I spot Al Wiman, a St. Louis TV reporter. He's standing twenty yards from the emergency entrance where our family gathered to face the horrible truth Friday. Wiman covers medical stories for his station. He's waiting while a crew sets up a camera and lights in front of the building.

I stop the car and introduce myself as Mary Fleming's brother. Wiman immediately focuses his attention on me and asks what he could do to help me. I tell him about Dad's reward and ask how he can make his offer on the news.

"Your station will be getting a scoop," I say.

He explains that the media considers such requests more public service announcements than scoops, and for maximum effect family members make such an appeal at a press conference through all the local stations simultaneously.

I persuade Dad to make the announcement himself, because the ugly scar above my eye makes me camera shy. I also don't want my family to think I'm trying to grab the spotlight by going on TV. I don't want to tarnish my relationship with Mickey in any way.

I envy Dad, because he spoke to her the Sunday before she died. They discussed the car, and I'm sure she was happy that he was going to help her. The sound of her voice is only five days away in his mind. It seems like a year since I left her laughing on the front porch. As hard as I try, I can't remember if we spoke with each other after that.

In the bright lights of the press conference, Dad looks different. Emotionally exhausted. Nervous. Cooperative, yet lost when TV crew members tell him where to stand and not look at the microphone. He isn't the man I'm used to seeing.

We used to joke about Dad's hands. His skin looks like the leathery, wrinkled hide on a turtle's neck, and his fingers curve inward like vulture talons. His are hands made powerful from years of squeezing wire cutters, but at this moment, they are shaking. He appears to be harmless. Suddenly, I realize this is how most people outside the family see Dad—people who doubt us when they hear us talk about his rampages. "Not Joe!" they say. "Joe wouldn't do anything like that. How can you say such a thing?"

The man standing in front of the cameras, under the bright lights, is a humble, small, sympathetic figure.

How hard it would be to imagine him yanking chunks of hair out of his wife's head or bending her thumb backward until it snapped. Who would envision this five-foot-ten, 165-pound man loading a high-powered rifle, forcing me onto a living room couch one hot summer evening, pressing the cold barrel into my forehead, and warning me not to get up or he'd shoot me?

Are we at the same police station where they brought Dad the night Mom stood on the front porch between him and the riot squad on the street?

That night, I jumped off the couch and ran outside to witness justice. At last, they were going to shoot the old man down, but like always, he managed to control himself in time. She talked him into dropping his gun, before they handcuffed him and took him away. He was out of jail by morning, and we all behaved as if nothing unusual happened, because in the Fleming household, nothing unusual *had* happened.

Dad's sweating under the hot video lights, when Al Wiman asks him why he thinks offering a cash reward will help find his daughter's killer.

"Those animals out in the jungle will do anything for five thousand dollars," Dad says, shaking, yet staring defiantly from camera to camera. "Maybe one of them is on drugs and needs a fix. I really don't care what they do with the money. I just want my daughter's murderer caught. She was a straight-A student in school, and everybody loved her. She had *no* enemies that I know of. She was a girl that any father would be proud of."

There he is, the man we fear, attempting to get us exactly what we need—public empathy and sympathy—but I know the video lights and close-ups aren't revealing the real Joe, the man I know. That man would just vent his anger and not really help us.

By the time he finishes, his eyes are watery. He sniffles and blows his nose. He cried at Mickey's funeral Mass. I don't remember anything else about the Mass except that we were in a church, Mickey's casket was in the center aisle, and tears were running down Dad's face.

I'm still shaken, ten days later, when I start my new job. The killer is on the loose, and the responsibilities of raising a child have increased the stress between Charlene and me. I had hoped that my new job would take me away from the assembly line mentality of the toiletry company, but it turns out to be merely another assembly line, this time of laboratory analysts following routine procedures and performing repetitive tests and analyses on pharmaceutical products.

I don't have my bachelor's degree yet, but I replace a man with a Microbiology degree from the University of Missouri at Columbia. He was at the job nearly two years and was good at it—working sixty hours a week. I learn that my salary is considerably more than his, and I let the figure slip into casual conversation with fellow workers. It angers the other analysts, which causes my boss problems.

Topeka, Kansas, August 6, 1980: Tony takes barbiturates with alcohol and writes a suicide note. He attempts to kill himself at his sister's house, but only superficially slashes his neck. The self-inflicted stab wounds to his chest are not life-threatening. He loses consciousness and is transported to St. Francis Hospital.

Our department chief began a three-month maternity leave on my first day, passing management responsibilities to her assistant. He's sympathetic and patient, and he tries to console me the few times he finds me, standing in the laboratory, facing a corner wall. The department chief would fire me.

Topeka, Kansas, Thursday, August 7, 1980: 3 a.m. LaRette is released from the hospital into the custody of Shawnee County jail.

Harvey and Plummer question their suspect. LaRette waives his right to remain silent and admits partial responsibility for Mickey's death. He claims that after dropping Roberson off at work, he picked up a hitchhiker in Roberson's neighborhood. The hitchhiker asked LaRette to take him to the house of a girl who owed him money. LaRette drove the hitchhiker to a grocery store and parked at the edge of its lot, near some apartments. The hitchhiker entered one of the apartments.

LaRette claims he waited 15 minutes, began to worry something might have happened to the hitchhiker, and went to the front door of the apartment.

When he looked inside, LaRette saw the hitchhiker stabbing a girl who was covered with blood and pleading for her life. LaRette entered through the back door, and the hitchhiker ran out the front door.

The girl's throat had been cut, but LaRette says he wasn't worried much because she wasn't gurgling. He worried about stab wounds to her chest, and tried to apply direct pressure to stop the bleeding. The girl started fighting, and then broke away and ran out the back door. LaRette had her blood all over his hands and was scared, so he left through the front door.

Detectives Harvey and Plummer prepare to transfer LaRette to St. Charles. As a deputy sheriff advises the suspect of his extradition rights, LaRette exclaims, "I tried to choke her first but I couldn't. She promised not to scream, but she lied to me. I caused an 18-year-old to die."

Most people at work hear about Mickey's murder, and they try to comfort me, but one chemist rushes into my laboratory and begins a tirade against murderers, rapists, child molesters, and society's inability to rid itself of these plagues. He's more upset than I am.

"People like that should be tortured," he says, matter-of-factly.

He's agitated that I'm at work and not out hunting down Mickey's killer.

"You love your sister, right?" he says, cocking his head to the side like a dog questioning a particular sound or a command. "You should be ready to sit in jail for killing her murderer. No one would blame you. So what if you give up some of your freedom? Freedom comes at a cost."

"I'm not going to let hate become a passion," I say, while that blinding rage I thought I set aside begins fomenting hatred inside.

"I don't know how you can still be here at work while that maniac is running free," he says.

I say something to him, and immediately forget what I said. I might have just looked hard at him, but he stays away from me after that.

St. Charles, Missouri, Thursday, August 7, 1980: 7 p.m. Suspect LaRette waives his right to remain silent and tells a slightly different hitchhiker story in which the hitchhiker runs out the back door of the apartment instead of the front, as in the previous version. The officers relate what witnesses told them about the convertible circling the neighborhood. The neighbors had seen only Mary Fleming exiting via the back door. The suspect begins crying, admits there was no hitchhiker, and says, "I did it."

LaRette claims he meant to burglarize the apartment and entered through an unlocked rear door. He ran into the basement, and then returned to find Mickey wearing only panties and standing in the living room. He had a knife, grabbed her, and told her he didn't want to hurt her. He told her not to scream, that all he wanted to do was get the hell out of there. The girl agreed not to scream, and he let her go.

"She starts screaming, and that is when it happened," LaRette says. "She lied to me. She promised me she wouldn't scream. She was just like all the others. My wife and my mother-in-law always lie to me. If she hadn't lied to me it wouldn't have happened."

LaRette tells the officers he does not remember what happened after the girl started screaming, and that he left by the front door and went to Roberson's car. He asks for a pain reliever and is given aspirin, and then signs a confession.

On the evening of the thirteenth day, Charlene and I are on the couch watching the local news on TV— it's close to 10:15 p.m. For once, I'm relieved they aren't covering the murder story. Mickey's graduation picture has been showing up in the daily newspapers and every evening on all the local television news programs. I don't like her graduation picture. She was wearing a dreary dress with a plain flower pattern. Her long dishwater-blonde hair begins straight and then billows around her shoulders, making her face appear chubby. Her broad smile and intelligent eyes are absent, and she's smiling indifferently at something or someone off-camera.

The phone rings, and I pick up. It's Detective Plummer. They found the killer. His name is Anthony Joe LaRette Jr., and he's already signed a confession.

It takes me a few moments to catch my breath, and then I find the words to tell him how much I appreciate all the work he and Harvey have done for my family. He is only doing his job, he says.

I hang up, and Charlene and I embrace. Mickey's death threatened to overwhelm Charlene. Since the night we arrived from California, she and Mickey became good friends.

I grab the Yellow Pages, write down the numbers of all the television stations, and call one after another, telling them that the killer has been found. We change channels and watch as station after station makes the announcement, and show the awful graduation picture. One news anchor is handed a piece of paper live on the air, and he reads, "This just in. An update on the murder investigation of St. Charles teenager, Mary Fleming...."

I call family and friends, everyone I can think of.

I don't sleep that night.

The next day, people at work congratulate me. They're happy for my family.

The hate-filled chemist who approached me the other day enters my laboratory for the first time since I'd told him off. He starts telling me how the system will let me down.

"The piece of shit will get a few years in jail, and then he'll be free again," he says. "I'd try to get my hands on him and kill him if I were you."

"That's not only ridiculous, it's impossible," I say.

"You have to at least prepare yourself for his release," he says firmly. "Get yourself a gun and be waiting when the son of a bitch is set free—and if you don't get him right then, go hunting for him."

I wonder where all his rancor comes from. Is he pissed at his dad, or what? The anger that had subsided in me following LaRette's capture begins to resurface.

"What the hell do you know about killing anyone? You have no idea what I'm going through. You come in here and spew all this *crap,* and you don't know what the fuck you're talking about. Just get the fuck out of here and leave me alone!" I say.

"Just trying to help you out, buddy," he says, and he turns and walks toward his department. My "buddy" eventually leaves the company, and I no longer have to deal with him.

The authorities release Anthony LaRette's mug shot. His long, greasy, knotted hair springs from his head in snake-like tentacles like Medusa. A string of Band-Aids applied vertically over a thin line that runs straight across his throat gives the illusion that he's wearing a primitive necklace. He tried to cut his throat as police bore down on him. He had sliced Mickey's throat, but he mocks her with the phony job he'd done on himself.

A few days later, I receive one of nine identical twenty-inch by fifteen-inch packages that were mailed to Mary Michelle Fleming's parents and siblings. Each package contains the same framed color photograph of her. During the week she spent with a friend in Arizona a month earlier, the girl's father, a professional photographer, let the girls talk him into taking some glamour shots for fun. Shocked by the news of Mickey's murder, the man feels moved to give us a gift.

Mickey, vibrant and youthful, is the principal subject of the photo. With both hands, she holds onto a thick tree branch and leans backward from the upper left-hand corner. Her body bisects the photo at a forty-five-degree angle across the out-of-focus background.

She is wearing black slacks and a white, cotton, peasant blouse with long sleeves. The wide, open-necked blouse exposes her smooth, tan shoulders. Her sun-bleached hair drops straight down, and if she were standing upright, it would end in the middle of her back.

She is looking into the camera lens, the Arizona sunlight dilating her pupils and intensifying her stare. I am a little bothered that she is also wearing lipstick and mascara, but my little sister is growing up. Her hazel almond eyes are confident, giving no clues to what she is thinking.

I can't interpret her smile, her red lips slightly apart offering a glimpse of her white teeth. It is a Mona Lisa smile, impossible to read, which makes the pose even more interesting. She might simply be saying, "This is me. I'm at peace with who I am." The photograph captures Mickey's enigmatic quality.

She will always be that way to me.

St. Charles, Missouri, September 1980: From a cell adjacent to LaRette's, an informant assists police in stopping his elaborate plan to help his father, Anthony Sr., sneak a gun into the jail through a barred window and murder one of the jailers.

St. Charles police arrest Anthony J. LaRette Sr.

Mom won't return to the apartment where her youngest child was taken from her. Susie gets her own apartment, so my brothers and I move Mom to a suburb in St. Louis County.

Her new apartment has room for the piano, but I let everyone know that I want it as soon as I find a place for it. Mom wants to keep it, but tells me that I can have it if something should happen to her or if she moves and doesn't have the space for it. I'm not going to argue with her—I'll wait—but I want that piano as soon as I can get my hands on it.

The tragedy of Mickey's death puts my relationship with Charlene into perspective. Our marriage was falling apart before Charlene became pregnant, but we probably would struggle on senselessly for a couple more years. We divorce three months after Mickey dies, and Charlene insists upon returning to California with Megan, to be with her family.

I could fight her in court, but she needs her mother and sister to help her adjust to life as a single parent. We sign the divorce papers in October 1980. I empty our bank accounts, which don't amount to much, and borrow money from Dad. The money Dad lends me, combined with my savings, is enough to keep Charlene comfortable for a couple of months while she settles down and finds a job.

On Halloween, I drive Charlene and Megan to the airport. I'm doing the right thing, yet as I kiss Megan goodbye at the terminal, I realize I'm sending my ten-month-old daughter 1,600 miles away.

Megan has just started running into my arms when I arrive home from work excited to see her. Invariably, Charlene would have just fed her, and it always occurs to me after I raise my girl above my head and she spits up onto my face, that her mother has been saying, "Don't, Dennis! I just fed her!"

As I walk past the baggage claim and out into the cold parking garage, I hold in my mind the image of

Megan's bright blue eyes and curly blond hair, and the warmth of her soft plump cheeks on my lips.

The murder trial is nearly a year away, and I find myself alone in our one-bedroom, second-story flat overlooking busy, noisy Highway 40. I've dealt with Mickey's death, felt some relief when they caught LaRette. What is there to do now but await the trial and follow it, in case something goes wrong?

I try to brighten the kitchen of my flat and paint it orange with yellow trim—but it looks like a clown exploded in there. I am not going to let the sadness of losing Mickey push me toward alcohol or drug abuse. That would be the exact opposite of what I promised her. My friend Tony drinks responsibly, and we spend several nights drinking beer and talking about art, politics, sports, and women. He usually drives me home.

Charlene needs dependable transportation in Southern California, so when I hear that Mike is preparing to drive there to look for work, I pay him food money—he won't take any more than that—to tow and deliver my Toyota to Charlene. With the car gone, every few months I buy or borrow a different junker from Dad, and then trade some of those lemons right back to him.

Dad passes the time at a used car lot located at an intersection where four or five roads join a one-way traffic circle, in north St. Louis. Instead of circling prey like vultures, Dad and the other salesmen play poker and wait for suckers to land on the lot. Dad and his cronies help a buyer select a car that looks sharp, seems priced right, but has serious hidden problems—a lemon sold *as is*.

I'm embarrassed driving Dad's cars around, so I joke about it by naming them. An old white Buick, a creamy Plymouth Valiant that smokes, and a yellow Ford Pinto (a make known for exploding when rear-ended) become the Great White Shark, the Turbid Tuna, and the Combustible Canary.

LaRette's preliminary hearing is in November, four months after his arrest. Police increase security—two armed deputy escorts instead of one—because LaRette tried to escape last month. Plummer and Harvey testify about interrogating LaRette in Kansas on August 7. Plummer tells the court LaRette started crying and admitted stabbing Mickey, telling them that he didn't meant to hurt her.

They set a hearing for January.

In mid-December, I get a call from my former next-door neighbor, Anne. She invites herself over, which I think is dangerous, since I'm lonely and vulnerable, and I might do something stupid, like make a pass at her. We used to flirt with each other. Anne is married, and I consider her husband, George, a friend. What if I make a pass at her?

I'm smart enough to tell her why I'm reluctant to see her, and she assures me we'll be safe.

She comes over the next evening. We have a glass of wine, and Anne tells me she's concerned that I seem depressed, and she wants to check in on me. I appreciate knowing she cares, and I wish she wasn't married. We might have a chance at something.

She stops me as I walk her to her car and tells me her girlfriend, Pat, asked about me. Pat was at the funeral with Anne, so I tell her to thank Pat for me. Anne asks if she can give my phone number to Pat.

"You can give my number to all your attractive, single friends," I say.

If Pat wants to drop by or meet somewhere, I'd be crazy to turn her down. But I really don't think she'll call. She's too cultured to go for someone like me. Born in Canada, she moved to Rome, where she attended the only French-speaking high school there. Like her mother, a Canadian, Pat speaks fluent French, English, and Italian well enough to teach all three. Her father, a consul for the Italian government, transferred to St. Louis with its large Italian community.

Anne and Pat became friends while in college. Pat received her Master's degree in St. Louis and teaches English at an all-girls Catholic school. I figure she won't want anything to do with a 30-year-old, working-class divorce' still a couple of years away from his B.A. in Biology.

Anne goes home. I rinse out our wine glasses and forget about the possibility of dating Pat.

On Mickey's first birthday following her death, John Lennon autographs an album for Mark David Chapman. It is a copy of Double Fantasy, the first album Lennon has produced in five years. Lennon recently said that, at 40, he feels more content than he's ever been in his life. Later, Chapman shoots Lennon in the back four times in the entrance of The Dakota, an apartment building in Manhattan. I admire and respect John Lennon immensely, but it is hard to care about him right now. Mickey should be turning 19 today.

At a hearing in January 1981, our family sits in expectation as a St. Charles County circuit judge rules that LaRette voluntarily gave his statements to Plummer and Harvey in Kansas, and the confession is admissible as evidence.

LaRette takes the stand and claims he'd been without sleep and hadn't eaten for three or four days when he gave his statements to Plummer and Harvey. He implies that he was so tired that he confessed to a murder he hadn't committed. He says they gave him painkillers for the wounds he inflicted to his neck and chest, suggesting he was under strong medication, and didn't realize what he was saying.

However, Plummer and Harvey both testify LaRette was alert and unaffected by any drugs he may have been given.

The prosecutor reads from the official record—the painkillers in question are aspirin. I hear someone joke, "I murder people when I take aspirin on an empty stomach, don't you?"

We laugh nervously, and someone says, "Pathetic."

The prosecutor asks LaRette if anyone forced him to make the statements.

"In a manner of speaking, yes," LaRette says. "They told me that if I'd tell them the whole story and it checked out, I'd be on my way home." Then he repeats the story of how he promised to let Mickey go if she promised not to yell out, but she lied. "That's when it happened. She lied to me, just like my wife and mother-in-law," LaRette had told Plummer.

An attractive brunette about 25 years old quickly rises and leaves the courtroom. Her look of indignation tells me she's LaRette's wife "the liar".

Over the course of the trial, LaRette uses many objective expressions to describe the brutal murder. He says, "That's when it happened," as if he'd only been a casual observer; "I panicked," as if he was more afraid of Mickey than she was of him; "I had no choice," as if he had been ordered to murder her; and "I did it," instead of "I killed her."

I would rather listen to him tell the truth as he really saw it, the way he'd boast about it. "Yeah, I killed her. I followed the cunt into the apartment to fuck her. She said she'd let me do it if I let her go, but she lied, so I stabbed her hard, right in her heart, but that wouldn't shut her up, so I smacked the bitch's ugly, screaming face and stabbed her again so I could get her clothes off and fuck her before my cock got soft. She got up and ran into the kitchen, but I caught her, and I slit her throat. Then the cunt grabbed the phone! Everything happened so fast I wasn't sure if the phone rang, or she answered, and somebody heard us. I threw her on the floor, and yanked her panties off. I wanted to fuck her alive, but she was squirming and bleeding all over the place. She was a goddamn mess. Somebody *had* to hear all the yelling. I had to get out of there fast. She went and died on me. I could have fucked her anyway, but I had to get out of there."

We don't hear these words. They're too close to the truth, too close to the real LaRette, or *LaRat* as we nicknamed him.

During one of the breaks, Susie and I leave the courtroom, when one of her girlfriends borrows my cigarette lighter. She's pregnant, in her eighth or ninth month. Susie takes me aside before I can congratulate the girl, and whispers, "Don't say anything about her baby, Denny. She lost it."

94

"She lost it?" I ask. "She looks like she's going to have it any minute."

"They only told her this morning—the baby is dead. They're going to take it tomorrow. It's better not to say anything about it."

The loss of another young life seems to pour more darkness into an afternoon filled with talk of murder and rape. The prosecutor comes out of the courtroom and asks Susie if she'll look at photographs of Mickey taken at the hospital. He wants to prepare her because they are going to ask her to look at them during the trial.

We sit on a bench together, but I can't look at the pictures. As badly as I wanted to see Mickey at the hospital the day she died, I don't have the strength to see her now. What if I lose control? LaRette is in the other room, and I might try to get to him. Anything can happen. Someone might be shot during all the commotion. Besides, the doctor at the hospital was right; I want to remember Mickey alive and vibrant, laughing at me making a fool of myself for her.

Susie examines the pictures of our mutilated sister with the same stoicism and courage she showed when she led the police through Mom's apartment.

Later, Dad quickly marches by as if on a mission, so I follow him through a corridor. It leads to LaRette. Two officers escort him outside to the front courthouse steps.

Handcuffed and wearing leg irons, he stands waiting for the paddy wagon to take him back to the city jail. Dad knows people who know other people, and he knows how to set things up. So, it doesn't surprise me when the officers standing beside LaRette and holding his arms step a few feet away from him, as if *he* needs space. He stands there bound and unprotected.

Suddenly, Dad pulls a single-edge razor blade paint scraper from his pocket. He pushes out the blade and whispers over his shoulder to me, "Watch me take care of this motherfucker."

Dad has arranged his window of opportunity, and he's going for it. A lifetime of snipping wires with wire cutters have given Dad a handshake that can make you cry, and I know that he will come close to severing LaRette's head—but I grab his arm, struggle with him, and hold him back.

"Don't, Dad!" I said. "He isn't worth it."

"I've lived my life. Let go of me," Dad says, as his window slams shut. One officer takes away Dad's razor and frisks him, and then returns to the other officer at his place beside the killer.

We wait for the wagon, and I'm still shaking from Dad's outburst. I carefully move into a position where I can stand face to face with LaRette. He looks past me at first, but then I make contact with his dead eyes. They could be brown, blue, or any variation. I see dull, solid black saucers. I don't know what I'm going to say, and

I'm afraid I'll burst into tears, but I won't have him see that.

"You killed my sister," I say.

"So what?" he says confidently, and smirks and shrugs, as if I just mentioned it might rain. He breaks eye contact and stands squinting slightly in the sunny afternoon. He is calm. His victims saw a different face. But he is already dead inside, and I think he knows it. I don't know what I expected him to say, but he's arrogant, as if it isn't such a big deal to murder someone, as if murdering someone is normal behavior. I think he's feigning confidence. He knows he's in deep shit.

The court judge sets the trial date for August and grants LaRette a change of venue to Warrenton, Missouri, a small town where we once lived for a year, when I was in the third grade.

Anne's friend Pat calls, and we arrange to meet at Anne's house in my old neighborhood.

Pat is 22 and every bit as refined in her mannerisms as she is refined in her speech. She charms me with her wit and mysterious dark eyes. I work up the nerve and ask her out, and we eat, serenaded by a mariachi band, at a Mexican restaurant. Then we catch a movie and talk late into the night about the film, art, philosophy—anything and everything. Every moment with her is imbued with a kind of hyper-cultural magic.

I drop her off at her apartment, and we kiss at her front door. I can't stop thinking about her the rest of the night. We continue to date, and for the first time in my life, I long to be with someone all the time. Our interests are in sync, and we spend hours discussing a book, film, or play.

She introduces me to my favorite novel, *Fifth Business*, by Robertson Davies. We read John Fowles' *The French Lieutenant's Woman,* and then see the movie, with Meryl Streep in the role of the complicated, sensual femme fatale. That afternoon, Pat and I make love in a passionate, erotic way I've never experienced before. We run dizzy and giggling one afternoon from a Georgia O'Keefe exhibit at the St. Louis Art Museum. I marvel at Pat's fashion sense and how it draws attention to her. She takes pride in putting together inexpensive articles to make ensembles that look as if they came from an expensive boutique. After six months, I move into her apartment.

On Friday, August 7, 1981, a sunny afternoon like the one when Mickey died, I leave St. Louis and drive two hours to the Warren County courthouse in Warrenton, Missouri, forty-five miles west of St. Charles. It's the first of many trips, and occasionally Joanie and Brian accompany me. We listen to music or engage in trivial conversation, avoiding the weight of the activity in which we are really engaged.

LaRette sits, heavily guarded, at the front of a courtroom. His hair is short, unlike the snake-like Medusa hair we had seen in his mug shot. The shallow scar around the base of his neck has faded, leaving no trace. Like a veteran actor waiting to go on stage, he gazes out into the audience, and actually seems to be enjoying the attention.

He is already a suspect in seven murders in and around his hometown of Topeka, Kansas. The patterns are similar. There are no signs of forced entry, and victims are raped and found stabbed in the chest with their throats cut.

He is alleged to have murdered and raped Tracy Miller while her 16-month-old daughter roamed the house unattended. LaRette's wife, Janet, a woman whose life has to be in constant turmoil, says that on the day Mrs. Miller was murdered LaRette came home, his hand wrapped in a towel. He'd been cut and was bleeding profusely. She thought it odd that he burned the towel that night. After viewing the design on similar linens found in the Miller home, Mrs. LaRette identifies it as the same pattern on the bloody towel that her husband burned.

Two women who had been raped in Manhattan, Kansas, describe a similar mark on the leg of the man who raped them—their descriptions match a birthmark on LaRette's leg.

LaRette sits at the end of a long table in front of the judge's bench. Though I sit near the back of the courtroom, I can clearly see his profile. Everyone can see his reactions to the heated exchanges between his defense attorney and the prosecutor. LaRette has a theatrical face with large expressive features. He listens, and comments with a shrug or a leer. Once again, society is victimizing him—an attitude he maintains throughout the proceedings.

A statement submitted by LaRette's mother describes her son as upset at the time of Mickey's murder because he found his wife having sex with another man in the backseat of a car. The prosecution ridicules the statement as an attempt to gain the jury's sympathy.

The hitchhiker story falls apart easily. Anyone else would have called the police or an ambulance to help the poor girl. Why didn't he? The prosecutor emphasizes LaRette's intent to kill, and shows the jury diagrams of the exterior and interior of Mom's apartment, saying, "He didn't come in there just to kill her. He cut her throat, tore her clothes off, and stabbed her twice in the chest as she was trying to get out the door." A medical expert testifies that Mickey would have bled to death from either chest wound.

The following Friday, August 14, 1981, the judge instructs the jury about specific guidelines that differentiate various types of murder convictions: second degree, first degree, and capital. The jury deliberates for about an hour, and then returns with the first of its two decisions—guilty of capital murder. This is *my* verdict. LaRette's face takes on a pale hue, and for the first time, he looks afraid.

A hint of relief works its way through my dulled senses. A capital murder conviction can have only one of two outcomes. He will either receive life with a minimum of 50 years before consideration for parole, or death in Missouri's gas chamber. A death penalty must meet the Missouri provision that "the offense was outrageous and wantonly vile, horrible, or inhumane in that it involved torture or depravity of the mind." At minimum, LaRette will get life, and will be out of circulation until he is 80. His life is over, and that is good enough for me.

The jury receives instructions on how to decide the second phase of their deliberations, the penalty phase, and then they leave the room.

We file out of the courtroom, and walk across the street to a small, neighborhood bar filled with locals talking loudly over jukebox music. Several locals offer their condolences when they overhear us discussing how quickly the jury returned with a guilty verdict. I order a burger as a bearded, elderly man in tattered bib overalls approaches our table.

"I'm sorry about what happened to your sister," he says loudly.

The chatter in the room suddenly lowers.

"We're farmers here. We got work to do. It'll comfort you to know that jury ain't gonna fool with that man. They ain't got time."

He points toward an open window that looks out onto an enormous oak tree standing tall on an empty lot next door. One large, horizontal branch about eight feet from the ground seems to point to the courthouse.

"See that tree? Last time we had a murder trial around here, that's the tree they finished it on. If we could hang him there, we would. They'll take care of him, though. Don't you worry."

The old man is right. The jury doesn't take long. In just over an hour later, we reenter the courtroom, where we see LaRette, reserved and expressionless, sitting up straight in his chair.

I take a seat even farther back in the room. The trial has exhausted me. It has exhausted us all. The jury enters and recommends the ultimate punishment—death.

An outburst of excited voices fills the crowded courtroom and is nearly stifled by one loud "Yes!" It's Joanie, and her voice carries equal parts anger and justification. I envy her. She'll finally be able to sleep. LaRette buries his face in his arms and cries.

Someone later says that he mumbled something about suicide. A rumor circulates that he's been advised to testify and reveal his history of mental illness, but he refuses, saying he doesn't want to go back to a mental institution. We didn't know he had a history of mental illness, but no one is surprised. A final sentencing date will be set later.

Dad wants to give the ⊠5,000 reward to police investigators, but they aren't allowed to take it.

A *St. Louis Post-Dispatch* reporter interviews Mom and Dad about the sentence. The headline reads: "Victim's Parents Differ Over Death Penalty." Quotes from both parents appear in the article. Dad drops his "animals in the jungle" metaphor and uses a poker analogy instead. "Actually, it's too good for him. He got what his hand called for." Mom holds a different view, saying, "I feel very sorry for him. I didn't want him to die. I'm going to pray for him."

I don't get the relief Joanie and most of my siblings and friends get from the death sentence. When it reaches my ears, I have no reaction comparable to joy or revenge. The guy is sick. They already decided to put him away for life. He'll never again kill or rape another woman.

I don't have a deep-seated need to see him dead, but I know that desire. I carried that deep and powerful hatred, but got rid of it because it contaminates my respect and love for Mickey. I pledge to honor her life by somehow turning something horrible into something positive.

It is a promise I mean to keep.

St. Charles, Missouri, October 7, 1981: Sixty-year-old Anthony J. LaRette Sr. is sentenced to six months in the St. Charles County jail for trying to help his son escape the same building a year earlier.

On October 8, 1981, after denying a motion for retrial, Warren County Circuit Judge Edward D. Hodge, an opponent of the death penalty, sentences Anthony J. LaRette Jr. to death by lethal gas. The date is set for November 16, 1981. I'm not in Warrenton for the final sentencing, but I read about it on the front page of the *St. Louis Globe-Democrat* under the headline: "LaRette gets Death Penalty in Stabbing of Young Woman."

Judge Hodge states that, despite his own philosophy, he won't impose his own opinion on the law, and it is his duty to uphold the Constitution. "I'm opposed to the death penalty. It brutalizes society. This person deserves it if anyone did," Hodge says.

Contrary to LaRette's tears and whispered threats of suicide two months earlier, he becomes angry and sneers at the judge and the assistant prosecutor.

In the picture accompanying the article, LaRette wears a dark leather jacket and a light shirt and tie as three officials lead him down a stairway. He's in handcuffs and leg shackles. His hair is short and trimmed, and he has a mustache. A uniformed cop clutches the murderer's right arm and a suited man has him on the left. A state trooper with sweat-stained armpits follows closely behind them. LaRette's looking down at the steps ahead. The article describes how a reporter tries to take the killer's picture, but LaRette lunges at the camera and pulls his escorts down beside him.

I read another headline near the bottom of the page: "Raped Girl, 12, Decides Not to Have Abortion." I wonder if they caught the rapist and whether he is her age or an adult. I can't bring myself to read any further. It seems as if a sickness of perversion is spreading.

One week later, LaRette files an appeal. I don't see how he can get out of his death sentence, unless they dig into his medical records, but he refuses to let them do that. He is probably going to die, and I have a feeling I will be there when he does.

Pat and I have been living together for more than a year, and the gloss of our infatuation with each other has rubbed off. She drives home to her family in Canada over the Thanksgiving break. I can't get away from work. When she comes back, she comes to a decision that, since we aren't going to marry, it's time to test the strength of our relationship. She says we each need our own space, which I take as the first big step toward a break-up.

So, I move out of her apartment and into a dreary one-bedroom flat in the city. I imagine my Uncle Bud wandering through the place, unaffected by the hideous wallpaper, its brown flower pattern yellowed with age, which make the walls look as if they are covered with 50-

year-old newspaper. A few drops of ether accidentally fell into one of Uncle Bud's eyes during a tonsillectomy in 1921, when he was 12, and he's been blind in that eye since then.

Pat drops by a few times over the next couple of weeks, but she won't stay long. I've been showing up unannounced at her front door, even though she asks me to stay away because my visits embarrass her in front of her friends. She never lets me in, despite my begging and, sometimes, weeping.

One night she comes by my place and cuts the cord. Even though I know it's coming, I take it hard anyway. The most passionate woman I've ever known, the woman I thought I was in love with—and who had asked me twice to marry her!—finally leaves me alone with nothing.

I'm in the middle of training for my second St. Louis Track Club annual marathon, and have been planning to enter the prestigious Boston marathon later in the year. I need to run the St. Louis event in two hours and fifty minutes to qualify. I entered the St. Louis marathon years earlier with no special training, running at my usual 7:22/mile pace, which brought me to the finish line in three hours and twelve minutes. For Boston, I'll have to shave off twenty minutes, and I think it is within reach. I've been running six to fourteen miles nearly every morning, and can cover ten miles in an hour. But when Pat dumps me, all that changes.

I start smoking and drinking with friends after work. Running becomes more painful each day, so I make a ridiculous decision. I'll blow out the first ten miles of the marathon in one hour, and after that, I'll pull back and run the next sixteen miles at just under seven minutes per mile.

It works for the first ten miles. I'm running like a champion near the top of the herd. By the thirteen-mile halfway point, I'm exhausted, jogging a few hundred yards, walking, and eventually sitting on a curb. I start walking off the course to quit, when another runner pats me on the back and encourages me to keep going. He points east. I can see the finish line.

Before the break-up, Pat promised me she'd be here—and the possibility she'll show up is the only reason I cross the finish line, stumbling over to an entry ramp at the St. Louis Cardinals baseball stadium, where the race started. I lean backward against a concrete wall, let my legs give out, and slide down to the sidewalk, scraping my back along the way. At least I finish.

"Can I get you something to drink?" asks Pat, as she bends toward me, hands on her knees.

"Thanks for coming," I say, shaking my head no. She congratulates me, and then leaves me sitting among the crowd of worn-out runners. My pace is a minute slower from the previous year—there will be no Boston.

I pay Pat one last visit, and give her the medal the track club gave me for finishing the marathon. She thanks me, and smiles condescendingly as if I'm a student who just gave her an apple. She returns to her apartment, but before she closes the door, I can see how quickly she re-engages in conversation with a group of friends, casting nervous glances in my direction. She carries the medal as if she just picked up the mail. I light a cigarette less than a block from her apartment and inhale deeply. I haven't eaten anything, and it nauseates me.

A friend at work tells me to pick up a copy of the March 1982 issue of *True Detective Magazine*. He says there is an article titled "The Naked Beauty and the Berserk Knifer," and it's about Mickey. "Look for the issue with the cute woman in a sexy pose hanging from a metal stairway," he says.

On my way home from work, I stop at a busy convenience store. I want to show the article to my family, and get the shock out of the way before any of them comes upon it unexpectedly. It seems impossible that the magazine has been out for a year, and we don't know about it.

I casually enter the store, not wanting to rush in like a vulture and grab the magazine. There it is on display between the tabloids and pulps. The cover photograph is surrounded by block-lettered captions: "Hog-Tied," "Rape Victim," "Homicide," "Killed By Her

Lover," "Crime Shocker," and "Murder" like the discount tags plastered on cheap bottles of perfume or liquor.

They staged the cover photo with a blond model around 20 years old who clings to the railing of an exterior fire escape not more than six feet above the ground. She poses with her red pumps planted on the landing in a kind of hanging squat. Her knees are higher than her ass, and the hem of her short dress gathers at the crotch revealing as much leg as possible for what is probably a PG-13 cover. A man wearing a police officer's hat and a blue short-sleeved shirt is supposed to be helping her down by grabbing her waist with his right hand. He has positioned his left to catch her butt when she lets loose.

As miserable as I am, I even envy *him*, his hands on a woman's ass.

I flip through the pages and find Mickey's senior photo—the same image that haunted all of us during the two-week hunt for her killer. My sister-in-law used to read *True Detective*. I'd find them lying around my brother's house, and I'd read a few articles. The crime scene details were explicit and always made me queasy. Seeing my little sister in a magazine like this puts a knot in my stomach. I consider stealing the rag rather than paying the ⊠1.25 to keep it in business, but I buy it.

I thought these magazines fake their stories. Though their accounts are supposed to come from real crime records, I always believed that publishers paid writers to dream up the scenarios. To my surprise, the story lays out the incidents and details of Mickey's murder exactly as they happened. The article describes how investigators interrogated more than seventy people, including friends, co-workers, teachers, and classmates, and arrived at the conclusion that Mickey "...was bright, attractive and popular, a woman without enemies, with everything to live for."

The article also shows one grim photograph of Mickey I've never seen. She's lying where she died on our neighbor's concrete front porch. Blood smears stain every part of the exposed concrete. She's been fitted with medical anti-shock trousers, balloon-like pants inflated to squeeze the blood from her lower extremities to her head to prevent oxygen loss in her brain. Her bloody feet are sticking out of the pant legs.

A small gas tank used to inflate the pants sits in the foreground. Five men are kneeling or squatting around her, courageously trying to save her life. A man in the left foreground is adjusting knobs on a control box that regulates the pants. On the right, obscuring Mickey's face, a paramedic is pressing down on her chest, trying to keep her heart pumping. Another man is tightening a belt on the anti-shock trousers. A stethoscope dangles from the neck of a man reaching into a medical bag.

The only person not wearing a paramedic shirt, the only man not busy, is squatting between the medical bag and the control box for the pants. He's wearing a white shirt and, though just a foot from the body, he is looking directly into the photographer's camera lens, staring right at me. He's probably a detective staying out of the way, perhaps hoping that she'll say something that will give him a lead. The look on his face says, "She's not going to make it." I've seen enough. If I could have been there. If I could have comforted her. If.

The article got the facts right, so it doesn't bother me. The magazine's readers will get a glimpse of what a wonderful girl Mickey was.

Mom wants to sue the publisher, so I call the police station downtown. They say it's a matter of public record, and we can't do anything about it.

March 29, 1983: Missouri Supreme Court affirms LaRette's conviction and sentence.

The world outside my apartment teems with people sharing their lives in meaningful conversation, or laughing, or running errands, people living with purpose. I'm a walking sense of dread, and mostly stay inside where I'm walled in by the rust-colored wallpaper, which begins peeling and emitting an odor that my microbiologist's senses tells me is mold. The lack of furniture makes the apartment seem larger than it is— spacious and empty, just like me. At night, the old darkened hardwood floor gives me the impression that I'm standing in a void.

An oil portrait of Pat hangs on the bedroom wall. A friend of her family, a successful sculptor named Rudolph Torrini, tried his hand at portraiture, and Pat volunteered. There are days when I think it is ugly, and others when I think it's okay—but I can't throw it away, or send it back to her. It is in a strange way company.

Breakfast, which has always been my favorite meal of the day, makes me sick. I usually eat big breakfasts, medium-sized lunches, and small dinners, but for some reason, breakfast has begun to disgust me. Eggs smell rotten. Fresh milk smells sour and ruins my cereal. The steam from a bowl of oatmeal seasoned with butter and brown sugar makes me want to throw up. Cinnamon toast tastes like gritty straw. I'm losing weight.

Running is boring, and taking a shower after a run fails to refresh me. I can't remember the last time I had an erection. Movies that end happily make me sad. I read and reread procedures at work, fearful I will botch a test. I can't get past the first few sentences in a news article, and I can't even start a novel.

Jokes aren't funny, and talk of birthdays and weddings, baby showers and housewarmings, keep me out of the work lunchroom and away from the water cooler. Any colleague's good news makes me jealous.

I go to bed early and exhausted, and over the counter sleeping pills fail to put me to sleep. I awaken after a few hours still tired, too early to get up, but too late to try to go back to sleep. So I lie there in the dark, wondering what is the point of living.

I think of suicide, but I always cling to the idea that things will get better. Besides, I don't have the guts to do it.

This morning, before I get out of bed, I've had enough, and I decide to kill myself.

I have to act fast or I'll back out. As soon as my feet hit the floor, I have to rush into the kitchen, grab a heavy carving knife, place the tip under the left center of my rib cage, and then, holding the handle firmly with both hands, shove the knife as hard and deep into my heart as I can. If I hesitate, I'll blow it.

I wait until I am absolutely sure that, once my feet hit the floor, once that cold floor stings the warm skin of my soles, I'll carry out the plan, as if ordered by a drill instructor. Fuck it, just do it.

I jump out of bed, run into the kitchen, and head directly for the drawer containing the knife, but as I do, I run into a familiar photo of my daughter, Megan, her blue-green eyes and golden hair practically blinding me.

The image hangs, suspended in the air directly in front of me. *Where did this come from?*

She's crying. I never noticed she was sad in that picture, but I'm not looking at a photograph. It is an image, a mental image as clear as a photograph directly in front of my face, and she saves my life.

I think of her growing up with the knowledge that her father killed himself, a father she hardly knew. I can't die after seeing that image. My daughter sees me very little as it is. I can't leave her with nothing.

I have a reason to live, and I realize I need psychological help. I'm paying child support, living on my own, and still making payments on the car I sent to Charlene. I can't afford a therapist, so I go to the V.A. hospital, fifteen minutes from work.

I tell an intake nurse about my disinterest in eating and my thoughts of suicide, and she books me an appointment with a psychologist named Dennis Dalbey. Dr. Dalbey puts me on a schedule of weekly visits and sedatives to relax me and help me regain my appetite. He says I have to get my body healthy before I can become emotionally healthy, so he starts me on Valium and eventually moves me to Librium. Since Dalbey's a psychologist, he can't prescribe, so he has to get an M.D. from across the hall to write my prescriptions.

The medication makes me sleepy, but I become less anxious and my appetite returns. We never talk much about Mickey. Instead, we focus on why it hurts so much to lose Pat. She and I never planned to make our relationship permanent. I turned down her marriage proposals. In light of all that, the fall I took when she dumped me seems far too hard, the depth of my depression too deep.

For nearly a year, I'm unfocused at work and live in a mental fog.

October 11, 1983: U.S. Supreme Court denies LaRette certiorari—a review of the decision of the lower court.

Mom calls. She's moving into a second-story flat in the city in order to be closer to work. I ask her not to sell the piano, to wait while I locate a truck and a few volunteers to move it into my apartment.

During the next few weeks, she asks me several times to come and get it.

"Let me know when you've reached the point that I absolutely have to take it," I tell her, "and if nothing else, I can put it in storage."

A few days later, Joanie calls and tells me that Mom settled into her new apartment—without the piano. We know Mom sold it, so I pay her a visit.

She has a new sleeper sofa—a fuzzy, plaid thing that I suspect has been purchased with piano profits. I promise her that if she tells me the truth, I won't tell anyone. She admits selling the piano, but refuses to tell me who purchased it. I try to reason with her, and make her see that whoever bought it will understand why the family wants to keep it. Technically, it was a gift from Dad, so it isn't Mom's to give away. She won't disclose the buyer.

The idea that she sold the one family keepsake infuriates me. I tell everyone anyway, including Dad. A few days later, Mom calls. He broke into her apartment, and tried to beat her. He was so drunk, she easily pushed him back down the stairs and into the street. I call Dad, and threaten to put him in the hospital if he doesn't stay away from Mom. Threats are all he understands.

Throughout most of Joanie's adulthood, she and Mom have remained close. They occasionally dine out on weekends, see movies and plays, and drink together. They are the bedrock of the family structure.

Mom always holds Christmas Eve dinner at her place. Cousins I never see all year show up, usually unexpectedly. I smile, slip some cash into envelopes, and then hand them out as if I have been waiting for them.

Joanie always arranges for Thanksgiving at her house, and we are all grateful because she is a great cook. She keeps the holiday meal restricted to immediate family and ever-changing significant others. The piano incident ends all that, and neither Joanie nor Mom ever again appear at the other's holiday gathering.

"Of course she sold the piano," Joanie tells me on the phone one day. "Haven't you learned by now? She doesn't care what it means to you or me. She only wants the money,"

It's harsh, but Mom deserves it, doesn't she? How can she sell the piano? It is the most important item in my relationship with Mickey. Mom's principles are nonexistent when money is involved—and from the moment she sells the piano, she becomes nonexistent to Joanie. No phone calls, visits, or invitations. Joanie already hates Dad. Now, she's orphaned herself.

December 21, 1983: LaRette files Rule 27.26, a motion for post-conviction relief.
June 12, 1984: Motion for post-conviction relief denied.
July 17, 1984: Notice of appeal filed.

A year goes by, and the silence between Joanie and Mom never breaks. Dad stops by Mom's apartment one afternoon, and they argue over the piano through the screen door on the front porch. She threatens to call the police the next time he comes over.

"The next time I see you, I swear you'll be in a coffin," he tells her, before driving away in the blue clunker we call his "Birdmobile."

Dad has a hook nose, and someone stuck him with the nickname "Beak." As he grew older, and his threats of violence became less terrifying, *we* began calling him Beak or the more demeaning Jodo, after the infamous extinct dodo bird.

Shortly after Dad's death pledge, Mom's doctor diagnoses her with lung cancer, and gives her six months to live. She calls Dad.

"Remember what you said about the next time you'd see me? Well, I'm going to make your wish come true, Joe."

She accepts the disease with humility. I never see her break down over it—but the diagnosis does nothing to change Joanie's attitude toward her.

"Now she thinks everyone will pity her," Joanie says. "Poor Millie—well, she's not fooling me."

I try to talk some sense into Joanie, but she won't listen. I call her one night, and though I plead and weep, she refuses to meet with me to discuss it.

"Come on. Mom's dying," I say. "You can bring real joy to her by simply walking into her hospital room. That's an incredible gift. She's in pain and doesn't have long to live. Can't you put aside the piano for that? I did."

Joanie won't budge.

"She's the ultimate martyr now. She thinks everyone will *have* to feel sorry for her. Well, she's going to die without *my* pity," she says.

Someone once said that love fades, but hate lasts forever. Nothing I say, nothing her husband says, nothing anyone says can change Joanie's mind. Anyone in Mom's condition, reduced to a physical body experiencing intense pain, deserves my sympathy.

Then I realize I've been a hypocrite. I let my emotions—my anger at Mom and my desire to make her suffer for selling the piano—take hold of me, and they led to more hatred. I told everyone what Mom did, and it set off a chain reaction of anger. Joanie went ballistic, and Dad found yet another reason to humiliate Mom. Even Brian has been bugging her about who bought the piano.

I move to an apartment to be closer to Mom. Susie, Mark, Brian and I drop by in daily rotation to check on her. Mom asks me to take the Virgin Mary planter off her hands.

"I know you like it," she says. "Besides, I can't get that little plant to grow, no matter what I do. Maybe you'll have better luck."

She's dying, but she wants me to give life to something. I never give plants the care they need. Someone once gave me a cutting, a simple green leaf, which I kept in water. It grew well until the water turned foul, and I couldn't put up with the stink. Eventually, even minimal care was too much, and I threw the reeking, rotting mass into a dumpster. In college, I skipped botany in favor of zoology and microbiology. Plants have never interested me.

I take home the Virgin Mary planter with its green four-inch plant and its thin leaves. I water and fertilize it, but nothing happens. I move it to several locations, trying to give it optimal sun, but nothing happens. So, after a couple of months, I leave it on the floor near the front door and forget about it.

Some of us are concerned about whether Mom fully understands that she isn't going to recover. I volunteer to tell her, and raise the subject one afternoon as I drive her home following a radiation treatment. She spots a donut shop, and asks me to stop and pick up a dozen. I park the car, and decide it's time to quit avoiding the subject.

"I have to tell you how serious this is, Mom," I say, waving away the few dollars she offers for the donuts.

"I know how serious it is, Denny."

She opens her purse and withdraws a small, plastic bag with a miniature blue logo. It's a tissue dispenser about twice the size of a matchbox. She pulls a tiny white tissue from a slit in the top of the bag and soaks up the tears collecting on her bottom eyelids. She says something about sharing the donuts, and tells me what kind she wants, but what I hear in my mind is that dreaded *word*. I know it has to come out—but I also know that once it's out, it isn't going to go back in.

"What are you waiting for?" she asks.

"Mom, do you understand what's going to happen after the treatments?" I still cannot bring myself to say the *word*. She offers me a tiny tissue, but it would be useless, so I use my shirtsleeve.

"I know I'm still going to be sick for a while."

She really *isn't* getting it. She glances at the store, still more concerned about getting donuts.

"How long do you think that's going to be, Mom?"

"I know it's terminal, Denny," she says softly.

120

She finally said it. She let it out—*terminal*. Yet strangely, nothing changes. She apparently can't see the correlation between the end of her therapy and the end of her life.

"Get the donuts. We're just sitting here."

"It means it's going to kill you, Mom—soon—within months." She looks at me through a veil of tears, but she isn't sobbing.

"I'm not afraid, Denny. I'll be the first one to see Mickey," she says, and smiles with conviction. I don't fall into her lap as I had the day we buried Mickey, but I become that confused little boy inside, crying for my Mommy. I thought I was going to be strong, but I'm unable to handle such powerful emotions. Mom gently pats my shoulder as I wipe away the tears streaming down my face.

"Go on, get the donuts."

"I can't go in there like this," I say.

"Ah, hell," she says, shutting her purse with a conversation-ending snap. "If anyone says anything, tell them you have a cold."

She still sees me as her child. She understands everything—and she is at peace with it. Mom hasn't been shrinking from the truth as we've been thinking. She's facing it gracefully, and it has made her wise. I enter the store, armed with my cold alibi.

During Mom's battle with cancer, she keeps her promise to Dad, and refuses to talk to him. She spends her last few weeks hospitalized in a morphine haze. Dad tries to call, but she insists she will die without him.

Susie wakes me with a telephone call Saturday at 2 a.m. She has been with Mom all night, and Mom just died. I'm upset that Susie has waited until after Mom passed to call me.

"It's something you don't want to experience if you don't have to, Denny," Susie says.

I've heard that something inexplicable happens when someone dies. They say death has an odor, or you can perceive something in the room, or see a change in the dying person's eyes. Whatever happens, it's a natural phenomenon, so why wouldn't I want to be present? Death is a part of life. I don't think Susie should make the decision for me, but she and Joanie have worked in nursing homes and have seen a lot of people die. I appreciate that I've been spared the anguish, but I feel cheated.

Later that day, my post-Pat girlfriend, Lori, and I leave our apartment to make Mom's funeral arrangements. I say something about how Mom is finally where she wants to be—with Mickey. It's a nice sentiment, but I don't really believe it.

Unpleasant as it is, I walk with little emotion through the preparations for the funeral and burial. They evoke the agony of making Mickey's arrangements three years ago, but in Mom's case, we all knew she was dying. She even arranged for a burial plot next to Mickey's.

Lori and I entertain Brian, his wife, Diane, Susie, and her husband John. We have a few drinks and talk about everything, so it seems, except Mom. Lori is sitting next to me on the couch when she seizes my arm and points at the Madonna planter.

"Look over there!" she says, trembling with fright.

Susie turns around, looks at the planter, takes a slow drag off her cigarette, and says to me, "You finally got that thing to grow, huh, Denny? What'd you do to it?"

Lori wraps her arm around mine and holds me close. We walk from the couch over to the planter, and I point to the foot-long stems and two-inch broad leaves. I make a four-inch spread with my forefingers. "This plant was only this tall on Saturday morning."

The room glows with the same soft white light I saw when my daughter's mobile spun that day after Mickey died. I can recognize Mom's presence—the way she finger-twirls her hair and chews ice cubes while she reads, the way she stokes a cigarette like a furnace before putting it down.

Through that little plant, I know that Mom is telling me she is finally with Mickey—and it fills me with an indescribable sense of calm.

Lori, on the other hand, spends the rest of the night waking me up to talk, to hold her, or to escort her to the bathroom. We're less than two years into our relationship, and a ghost has entered our home—one she isn't as familiar with as I am. I keep thinking what Mom told me at the donut shop: "I'll be the first one to be with Mickey."

The little plant is the second spiritual event associated with Mickey's death.

The next day, I take the planter to Mom's funeral Mass. She regularly attended Mass, honored holy days, and took the sacraments. Dad tells the priest about the plant's miraculous growth spurt, but he isn't as impressed as we are. In the scheme of miracles, I suppose it's insignificant.

So, I set the planter beside Mom's casket, and glance at it occasionally, paying little attention to the service. Instead, I reflect on good memories of Mom.

I remember her drawing me out of warm, milky bath water and standing me on a furry toilet lid, wrapping a fluffy white towel around me, and with a gentle hug, squeezing my warmth into it. She smelled like peaches. After patting me dry all over, she ruffled the towel through my hair. I felt all aglow and loved. Her red lipstick had smeared from kissing me. She told me I had the most beautiful blue eyes and soft skin. I heard the gurgling of the draining bathtub, a soft, shallow sound changing to a deep, hollow echo fading into a silence that brought a feeling of absolute safety and bliss.

Somewhere along the line, I lost sight of Mom's simple, good-natured spirit. When we still believed in Santa Claus, she created magic for us each year between Thanksgiving and Christmas—her baking season. She filled the house with the aroma of butterscotch, vanilla, and chocolate. On her pie crusts, on the tops of cookies, and in the cake icing, we found footprints of tiny elves. Santa's helpers, Mom said, tiptoed around during the holidays watching and evaluating us. The elves could make themselves invisible.

Now and again we would hear Mom talking to someone in the kitchen, and then she'd yell, "Hurry up, kids! An elf is stuck in the icing. Quick, before he climbs out of the bowl! Hurry!" We'd dash into her warm kitchen, but always too late. "Oh, you just missed him," she'd say, frustrated that we always arrived too late, but there in front of us, we could see the evidence—tiny tracks in the dark chocolate icing at the bottom of the mixing bowl.

"Did you feel anything, like a wind against your face?" Mom would ask. "That's his sleigh passing by."

That tiny wind brushed against my face, so slight that it *had* to be an elf sleigh.

The holiday season was Mom's special time. It was her chance to give us a real childhood and to help us forget the one Dad usually took away when he arrived, and sent us into hiding.

Joanie doesn't attend the funeral, which makes no sense to me because funerals aren't so much to honor the deceased as they are to comfort those mourning.

Dad gets his wish of seeing Mom in a coffin, but he pays a heavy emotional price. A friend of mine from work sees him in the funeral parlor lobby and asks, "Who's the old man sitting on the steps in the lobby? He looks sick. He's awfully pale."

"That's my father," I say.

During one of my weekly visits to see Dr. Dalbey, I take the usual stairway to his third-floor office. An unfamiliar receptionist greets me, and sends me to a waiting room. I've been seeing Dr. Dalbey for over a year, and I've always gone straight into his office.

About ten people are waiting in the small room. I take the only available seat next to a man who needs a shave and smells like old floor wax. A strange vagueness seems to hang in the air. No one is reading a magazine. A woman in a faded, blue, thin cotton dress is picking pieces of paint from the wall and closely examining them. The pungent man next to me asks if I have a light for his cigarette.

"No, I don't. Sorry," I say. "Do they allow smoking in here?"

He launches into a monologue, jumping from one topic to another with no correlation between subjects. He mentions early TV shows, current events, and comic books. Have I noticed hairstyles lately? The entire time, an unlit cigarette dangles from his mouth, and he repeatedly interrupts his blather to ask me for a light.

After the sixth or seventh request, I look him straight in the eye and firmly say, "No!"

He slowly draws back, looks at me as if I am the one out of my mind, and lights his cigarette with a lighter he pulls out of his pocket. Meanwhile, the woman in the faded dress kneels and continues inspecting the wall.

I leave the room, and ask the receptionist if she will contact Dr. Dalbey and find out when I can see him. She looks at a scheduling chart, and then asks me to wait a minute while she makes a call.

"Dr. Dalbey's not on this floor," she says, "but he'll be right down." I wait at the desk a few minutes until Dr. Dalbey comes grinning down the hallway.

"They are waiting for their monthly injections," he says as he leads me past the waiting room and upstairs to his office. I wonder if I will end up waiting for a monthly shot some day.

I'm in what I call my *gray period*. I am not aware of the depth of my depression—even though an attempted suicide initially drove me into therapy. My world is colorless. I can't visit an art museum or see a film that interests me—everything is ugly.

The sessions with Dr. Dalbey help me see a link between my depression over losing Pat and losing Mickey. In the midst of the family turmoil brought about by alcohol and drug abuse, violence and hatred, Mickey had been my island of stability. Whenever I had a chance to say "I'm her brother," I felt a sense of pride—not the usual emptiness, twinge of embarrassment, or shame I felt about my parents. I had put my grieving aside and focused on Pat. She filled the hole in my heart left by Mickey's death.

Dr. Dalbey lights a cigarette, and then offers me one, which I refuse. I haven't smoked in months. I begin to realize that something fundamental is missing from my life, and it isn't cigarettes.

"She was like having another part of myself in the family—a better self," I say.

"You identified with her, with her potential."

"If Mickey and I were alike, she was a much better version of me."

He takes a long drag on his cigarette and folds his arms. Then he leans back in the chair and puts his feet up on his desk. I have a feeling he's going to say something that is going to piss me off.

"Have you ever thought about what your sister might be like now if she lived?"

"I figure she'd graduate from college and be a professional of some sort. Why?"

"You have these wonderful feelings for Mickey, and you *should* have them. I don't know whether you've considered that, had this terrible tragedy not occurred, if Mickey had lived, what twists and turns her life might have taken."

I know what he's getting at. Any number of things could have gone wrong in Mickey's life. She might have succumbed to the environment around her. She might have wasted her talents.

"I know I'm probably idealizing her, but no one knows the future. Why not imagine the best?"

"Are you angry with me?" he asks.

"No. Why?"

"Does it bother you that my name is Dennis, too?"

I never gave it much thought. Of course, I noticed that his name is Dennis. It seems absurd that he's asking if it bothers me. I start laughing, and the more I look at him, the more I laugh. He begins to look like a cartoon—like a tan Elmer Fudd with a bad toupee.

"I'm sorry. I don't know why I'm laughing," I say.

"Don't be. You can laugh at me. I don't care what you think of me."

"What if I quit therapy because I just don't like you?"

"I wouldn't lose any sleep over it."

Now I *don't* know what he is getting at, but it felt good to laugh. I haven't laughed in a long time.

"This might sound crazy," I say, aware of the irony of using that phrase in a psychologist's office, and laughing even more.

He takes his feet off the desk and leans forward in his chair.

"What is it?"

"What I'd really like to do is go to an island or a mountain somewhere. Live in a Zen monastery until I discover my reason for being—my true calling in life."

"Who you are is more important than what you do. You need to explore who you are. What you want to do will come," he says.

"But that's what I'm having trouble with. How do I explore who I am?"

"Well, there's the paradox. You can find out who you are by exploring things you really like to do—fun things, enjoyable things."

I tell Dalbey I read an article about how a person could get an idea of what they really want by imagining their success in any endeavor being magically guaranteed. Nothing the person tried could fail.

"What would you do?" he asks.

"Something to do with acting and film—maybe comedy."

He suggests I think of it as a hobby, check some books out of the library, or enroll in a class.

"Hobbies are for miniature train or stamp or coin collectors. I've never had a hobby, except maybe running," I say.

"Have some fun with it," he says.

When I leave the session, I take the stairway I always use. Each landing is white and nondescript, but how did I miss an entire floor?

Lori and I break up, and she moves out, so I have plenty of time. Without a specific plan, I set out to do what I like, not what I think I should like. Years ago, when I left the Corps and entered the University of

California, logic told me to major in science, rather than in the arts. I primarily read books to improve my work or enrich me culturally, books I felt I was supposed to read. After my talk with Dalbey, I begin reading books I *like*.

I read and attend plays: Shakespeare, Sartre, Pinter, Mamet, and Beckett. I enroll in an acting class and see live plays and plays on film. I become interested in movies with intense psychological themes, powerful characterizations, and a strong visual language, particularly foreign films. I seek out the work of film directors who use the medium as an art form as well as for entertainment: Cassavetes, Scorsese, Coppola, Kurosawa, Polanski, and Godard. Overwhelmed by *Apocalypse Now*, I am unable to describe it to a man who stops me in the theater parking lot and asks me if the film is any good. Fumbling words, I finally say it is a work of art—maybe even a masterpiece.

I see most of my films at the Tivoli Theater, an arthouse in the hip Delmar Loop area of nearby University City. On the way to the Tivoli, I often pass another theater, the Varsity. Although it's only a couple of blocks west, I've never seen a film there. The Varsity runs horror films, strange movies, and midnight films I've never heard of and have little interest in seeing. *The Rocky Horror Picture Show* plays there regularly and draws large crowds, dressed like the movie's characters, who sing along with the film in a kind of theatrical karaoke. I am interested in film and theater that explore

131

the boundaries of the art form and the human condition in more subtle ways.

November 26, 1985: Missouri Court of Appeals, Eastern District, affirms denial of LaRette's post-conviction relief.

A poster announcing a midnight showing of a movie called *Eraserhead* never disappears from the Varsity's display windows for more than a few weeks before it's back on display. The movie runs for one or two weeks, disappears for several, and then returns. It is as if the film is so intense that the theater can't hold onto it for more than a few weeks at a time.

The *Eraserhead* poster's no more than a plain black-and-white photograph of a man in a black suit with a white shirt and a black tie. His hair, backlit by bright white light, is teased ten inches straight up, giving the subtle impression that his head is exploding. The look on his face, a blank stare, reminds me of LaRette. No one who has seen the movie can explain its story or plot other than to say that the movie isn't technically a horror film. Also, no one ever says it isn't worth seeing, so I'm going to see what makes it indescribable.

The theater is old and damp and in disrepair. At five minutes until midnight, with only three or four other people in the auditorium, I find a seat about two-thirds of the way back from the screen—an ideal place to sit.

The story turns out to be simple. The main character, Henry Spencer, is a walking definition of angst, a man standing inside his own nightmare. He exists in a state of continual, painful introspection, as if staring inside himself, confronting his fears, and surrendering to them.

During dinner at his girlfriend's house, Henry learns that she has given birth to a premature and deformed child—his child.

Henry takes his girlfriend, Mary, and the baby home with him to his one-room apartment. The baby cries constantly, creating an escalating tension that Henry tolerates, but Mary can't. His indifference to her agony drives her away, and she deserts them both. The baby becomes ill, and after Henry's failed attempts to ease its misery, he kills it.

Though the film's plot is uncomplicated, its power evolves from its stunning imagery and complex, multilayered soundtrack. Henry's sympathetic character (portrayed in a stunning performance by Jack Nance) takes the audience into a colorless neighborhood in a world held hostage by a cacophony of industrial sounds that add a foreboding subtext to the story. When Henry brushes lint from his pajamas, the magnified sound seems just as meaningful as the grinding metal, steam releases, and rumblings emanating from unknown sources in the industrial wasteland.

The movie is unlike anything I've ever experienced. I feel as if I am dreaming the entire experience, as if the movie has replaced the inner landscape of my mind, and then I have entered the movie's narrative.

Much of the film has a low budget student film quality—it is in fact a student film—but despite what would be limitations to most students, the young filmmaker, David Lynch, produces a beautiful cinematic masterpiece. I experience equal measures of horror and delight, love and hate, beauty and repugnance. If the film were a painting, it could hang in a gallery beside the works of surrealist and expressionist masters.

I leave the theater and enter a world outside that has changed. It has rained, and the wet streets and buildings reflect the black night of the 2 a.m. sky. Streetlamps reflecting in the storefront windows vibrate with energy. It's as if I am still inside the movie. If this director can do so much with so little, I have a real chance to make films myself. Nothing has ever inspired me so directly and powerfully. I decide to make a film for no other reason than that the thought of doing so excites me.

After several calls to universities and colleges around town, I find a class called "Sweet Dreams: Film, Freud, and Fantasy" at the Forest Park campus of the St. Louis community college system. The course is taught by R D Zurick, an eccentric artist and teacher who shoots and edits his own personal non-narrative avant-garde films. When I learn that he considers *Eraserhead* a masterpiece of surrealism and shows the film in his class, I sign up for an evening session.

April 11, 1986: LaRette files a petition for writ of habeas corpus in the United States District Court of Eastern Missouri.

October 9, 1986: LaRette files a second post-conviction appeal in Warren County Circuit Court, Warrenton, Missouri.

Most students in Zurick's filmmaking class create music videos by editing images to a favorite piece of music, but I want to make a film with actors, locations, and sound. I turn in a screenplay for a fifteen-minute short, an homage to David Lynch, titled *Mr. Dorman Lives in St. Louis.* I write a story in which a woman reflects on one particular day in her childhood when she sold Girl Scout cookies to a strange, perhaps frightening man who lived in a noisy industrial complex. It'll be interesting to see someone like *Eraserhead's* Henry Spencer through the eyes of a child. A co-worker and friend, Bob Schindler, agrees to play the part. He has seen *Eraserhead* and understands exactly what I want. A woman in my department lets her daughter play the part of the Girl Scout. The little girl comes complete with her own uniform.

I shoot and edit the movie, play harmonica for the soundtrack, and provide a voiceover. At 60 mph, I hold a cassette recorder out the driver's window of my car and record the rushing wind, which I distort at high volumes and use for rumbling industrial sound effects. I collect audio samples from pieces of equipment at work: centrifuges, autosamplers, test tube vortex vibrators, and bottle shakers. I do everything but act in the film. A local studio transfers the film to three-quarter inch production video, which gives me the flexibility to alter the visual contrast and the audio track, and to further edit the images.

Mr. Zurick invites me to several film classes to screen *Mr. Dorman.* Two local high schools invite me to show the film and then discuss it with students. Most people who've seen *The Elephant Man* or *Eraserhead* can see Lynch's influence on *Mr. Dorman Lives in St. Louis.* As a microbiologist by day, and a filmmaker by night, I develop a passion for motion picture art from which I gain a deep sense of fulfillment for the first time in my life.

On my way to see Dr. Dalbey one morning, I slowly notice that color is returning to the world: green leaves on brown trees, a blue sky, and cars so colorful that they look like big toys. Dalbey says it's a sign that I'm coming out of my depression.

A month later, we end two years of weekly therapy sessions, but Dr. Dalbey cautions: "It's extremely important to remember the depth of your depression. You can easily go back there."

Now I can identify my depression as a specific place where I've been trapped. I'm removed from it, and promise myself not to slip back into it.

November 30, 1987: Warren County Circuit Court denies LaRette relief.

July 26, 1988: Missouri Court of Appeals affirms Circuit Court's denial of relief.

After I show the film at a film festival at a local university, my new girlfriend, Chris—another highly cultured woman, a sort of German version of Pat—urges me to apply to the Tisch School of the Arts at New York University, even though my entire formal filmmaking experience is limited to one fifteen-minute student film. The thought of moving to a fast paced megalopolis like New York City terrifies me, but Chris has enough confidence for both of us. She earned her master's degree in Music Performance from the University of Wisconsin, and she loves to play her cello and teach. She spent her elementary and middle school years in New Jersey. Her parents recognized her musical talent and enrolled her in an on-going weekend music program at The Juilliard School in Manhattan. Chris says I have nothing to lose. I won't be expecting them to accept me, so why not see what happens?

Missouri State Penitentiary, Jefferson City, Missouri, October 27, 1988: Richard Lee and Chief Deputy George Brooks are investigating the murder of an elderly woman and her 40-yr-old son in Missouri's Cole County. They follow a trail of evidence that leads to Pinellas County, Florida.

Each year, the Cinema Studies program at NYU's Tisch School of the Arts receives about 500 applications from around the world to fill only sixty available spots. Forty students are directly selected from the current applicants. An additional twenty, identified the previous year as having potential, make up the full roster of sixty. They mark me as one of the twenty applicants who show potential and are almost certain to be accepted the following year. This is better than being accepted immediately, because Chris has enough time to find a teaching job at a prestigious school on Long Island. She's excited about the opportunity to gig around New York City, an artist's paradise.

I quit my job as a quality assurance microbiologist, and we prepare to move to Brooklyn. One thing, though—Chris insists that we get married. She had invested her years from high school through graduate school and beyond into her first marriage, but it turned out badly, and she isn't about to support me for three years without some type of guarantee. Imperfect as marriage is, she says it means more to her to be my wife than my significant other. Ours is a passionate, yet volatile relationship—we argue in the car on the way to our wedding ceremony, and I almost back out.

Jefferson City, Missouri, January 1989: Dr. A.E. Daniel, a consultant in correctional mental health and psychiatry, prepares a psychiatric evaluation of LaRette that includes medical records from 1959-1978. Conclusion: At the time of the murder LaRette was suffering from organic mental disorder due to partial complex psychomotor seizures or Temporal Lobe Epilepsy that provided a definite case of diminished capacity and was a strong mitigating factor that should have been introduced at the penalty phase of LaRette's trial.

Since Chris is helping me fulfill my dream to become a filmmaker, she wants me to help fulfill hers. Her father died of Huntington's disease, which means that his children have a 50/50 chance of carrying the gene that expresses the illness. Chris has waited to consider having children until she is nearly forty, an age experts say significantly reduces the probability that she carries the gene. If she doesn't have the disease, her children will also be free from it. She wants a child, and she wants it soon to reduce the risk of age-related first-birth complications. We agree to try, but even with a concerted effort, I guess we won't conceive for years. Within three months, Chris is pregnant.

Part III
Courage

Courage is not simply one of the virtues, but the form of every virtue at the testing point.
C. S. Lewis

We gain strength, and courage, and confidence by each experience in which we really stop to look fear in the face... we must do that which we think we cannot.
Eleanor Roosevelt

Pinellas County Sheriff's Office, Largo, Florida, February 1989: Pinellas County is large, with twenty-four incorporated municipalities including Clearwater and St. Petersburg, and the workload is heavy. Detective Patricia "Pat" Juhl works in the adult crimes section: homicides, suicides, suspicious deaths, and rapes. She receives a request for assistance from Jefferson City, Missouri. Detectives Richard Lee and George Brooks have information on a murder suspect who may have had connections to Pinellas County. Lee and Brooks fly to Largo, and Juhl helps them run down leads and interview people. With the information they obtain in Florida, Lee and Brooks are able to solve the Cole County double homicide.

Besides course study, a filmmaker has to make films, an extremely time-consuming collaborative activity. I'll be expected to spend any precious spare time helping others with their projects. If I fail to do that, who'll be there for me? It will be a full-time job that will frequently run late into the night or early the next morning. There'll be no time for a newborn. I don't see how I can manage it. I've been a long-distance Dad to Megan, flying to California several times a year and flying her to St. Louis when she got older. I'm not about to be so distant from my second child, so we stay in St. Louis. I wrote a solid six-minute script for the NYU admissions writing requirement, a betrayal-themed piece called *Brian's Lie*. The process of writing it has opened new creative energies for me. I'll stay in St. Louis and try to write a screenplay for a feature film.

Missouri State Penitentiary, Jefferson City, Missouri: Richard Lee begins a series of "small talks" with LaRette who begins volunteering information about a murder he committed in Pinellas County, Florida, in the mid-1970s. Lee coaxes LaRette into cooperating by granting special parental visits. Lee and tells LaRette that he knows a friendly little woman in law enforcement in Florida, and he'd like to do something nice for her. LaRette suggests, "Maybe we could do that. Maybe we could clear up some murders up there for her."

Juhl flies to Jefferson City to the state's antiquated penal institution. Carrying sidearms, Brooks and Lee accompany her to a conference room. "You have to remember two things," Lee tells Juhl. "One, this guy was a serial rapist. And two, you are one of the few women contacts he will have inside the prison."

LaRette enters in handcuffs. He is six feet tall and towers over the detective. As they are introduced, Juhl shows no reluctance to shake hands with the killer. LaRette provides pencil sketches of the crime scene and other specifics that match details of one of Juhl's unsolved homicides for which she has no physical evidence and no suspects.

Weeks after meeting Juhl, LaRette writes her a letter saying, "This letter is something I never thought I would do. I fought against your [profession] for so long. But I seen something in your eyes that first time. I seen in your eyes and speech that I could trust you somewhat. You are still the law and I know that you'll do your job. But there also is a heart in Pat that does care."

Using my *Mr. Dorman* as an example of previous work, I apply for a grant for an experimental film I title *Rest Room*—a story about an attempted suicide in a public restroom. I receive the grant, and I am able to pay actors and some crew members. I have a makeup artist, a script continuity person, a director of photography, a sound technician, about twelve people in all—a real film crew.

Inspired by nothing more than intuition, I edit the story so that it starts at the end, but then, instead of working my way backward, I insert the first scene followed by the second from the end and work my way back and forth into the middle of the story. The temporal reordering allows me to draw the audience into scenes unexpectedly. The suspense and tension of the work challenges viewers to put the whole story together in their minds and results in a wonderful final irony, which would be lost in a straightforward version. *Rest Room* runs on a local cable program, *Mind Over Television*, and an important St. Louis film critic gives it a positive review. I'm thrilled.

Mickey would be proud of me.

Potosi, Missouri, March 1989: LaRette is transferred to the newly-opened Potosi Correctional Center (PCC). An FBI profiler from Topeka, Kansas, is brought in to talk with him about his childhood in an effort to spot potential problems in children and prevent what happened to him from happening to others. It takes two days to get the killer to agree to the interview. During conversations, he does not reveal any murder details.

LaRette insists future interviews are to be held exclusively with Juhl.

On her second trip to Missouri, Juhl visits LaRette at the PCC. He describes, in detail, entering a home in Marathon Key, Florida, and choking a woman before repeatedly stabbing her with a knife, and slitting her throat.

Juhl establishes a working relationship with LaRette—a rare professional bond with a serial killer. She calls him Tony, and begins a process of corresponding with him through letters and his collect phone calls. He provides limited information on murders and rapes he's committed. "He tests me to see if I am really interested. He wants to see if I am going to check out what he is feeding me," says Juhl.

Once Juhl establishes the veracity of LaRette's specific case details, she flies to Missouri the night before a scheduled interview. She spends the next morning "warming him up," during which he updates her on his appeals and his routines and activities at the institution. They share experiences about Florida's parks and groves. LaRette refers to himself as "captain" because he likes the water and likes fishing off a pier at Fort DeSoto Park. Juhl finds that the killer converses easily and speaks well. She tells coworkers that most people wouldn't know LaRette was dangerous. In the afternoon, they get down to business. He provides the rest of the information he has, which frequently leads to closing an unsolved homicide or rape investigation.

In written correspondence describing crime scenes, LaRette frequently signs the bottom of documents and inscribes things like, "Young woman, 1979, 9pm-10pm, Rape".

One inscription includes the victim's height and weight and what LaRette stole from her.

In another letter, in which he reflects on his early arrest for indecent exposure, he says he didn't know why he was masturbating in public and wants to find out why. Juhl learns that he'd positioned some of his victims in a particular way, which became a trademark.

He pencil-sketches a portrait of Juhl and sends it along with a self-portrait to her. "The drawings are actually quite good," says Juhl.

My son, Sean, is born in June 1990. After Chris' summer vacation, she takes her maternity leave during the first three months of the school year, and then returns to work. We put Sean in infant daycare two days a week, and I stay home with him the other three. I begin working on a story idea for a feature film I title *Children of the Lie*. I take some film writing classes and seminars and manage to pick up a few writing assignments that pay.

My previous employer contacts me and hires me as a consultant. I can schedule my time as I see fit. It's too good to pass up, and it pays well. I left home at seventeen, and I've always taken care of myself and can't get used to relying on someone else to support me financially.

Juhl discovers that LaRette had roamed throughout eleven states in the Midwest and Southeast. He never held a steady job. When he ran short on cash and couldn't steal, he'd call home, and his mother—whom he held in high regard—would wire him money through Western Union. The killer believes he is a victim of his environment—sexual abuse, his mother's absence, and his father's cruelty.

He argues that his troubles began at birth. He thinks his mother's age—she was in her forties when he was born—and his abnormal birth weight of twelve pounds were the beginning of his mental and emotional problems. His mother worked all the time and was never home, and his father was an alcoholic. LaRette claims a babysitter repeatedly molested him, but Juhl cannot verify it.

LaRette claims that at eighteen he murdered his first victim, a man his age, during a fight in a car near a railroad track. His second and third homicides were simultaneous. He was raping a woman, and when her husband arrived home from work, LaRette murdered him as well.

He maintains he committed murders on beaches in Florida, but Juhl cannot confirm them, even though LaRette draws detailed pictures of the crime scenes. He'd steal work shirts and other clothing and impersonate repairmen in order to gain entry into homes. He spent time stalking his victims. Yet, in telling the stories, he always makes it seem as though something his victims did triggered the situation—forced him to murder them.

LaRette says he would become overwhelmed by rage, and that's when he committed the murders and rapes. He asserts that all of his killings were people he did not know, and he distinguishes between rapes and rape-murders. The killer gives Juhl no indication that he had a relationship with any of his victims, nor were any of them children.

He thought he left most for dead, but Juhl is able to establish that a few he'd thought he had murdered had lived. He raped and beat a woman in O'Fallon, Missouri, and threw her into a ditch thinking she was dead—but she survived.

Despite Chris' belief in me as an artist, our marriage stumbles toward its inevitable crash. I'm diagnosed with Bipolar Disorder during the process, but nothing can erase the emotional ugliness through which Chris and I continually put each other. We divorce when Sean is two, but I'm able to sustain a closer relationship with him than the one I had maintained with Megan.

During Juhl's third visit, LaRette elaborates on the information he originally supplied to Lee, which had brought Juhl to Missouri in February. He draws a map of a St. Petersburg woman's route home from her job at a nearby cemetery. He describes the layout of her home and the placement of Early American furniture and the shade of her carpeting. He confesses to killing her with a bayonet that he found hanging on her living room wall.

"I turned right toward the living room. The woman yells, ⊠What are you doing in my house?' I started running toward her, and she grabbed a bayonet," says LaRette, in a monotone voice, covering his mouth to hide his bad teeth.

"Sometimes he closes his eyes when he describes a murder. You could tell he was reliving it in his mind," says Juhl.

Upon reviewing videotapes of Juhl's interviews with LaRette, Marsha Baird of the Shawnee County Sheriff's Department, Topeka, Kansas, notes that LaRette never veered from a pattern. "Normally, Tony would look off to the side and down to the floor when he began talking about a crime. This mannerism was so consistent; it became one of the ways we could distinguish if he was telling us the truth and when he was embellishing a story," said Baird.

LaRette maintains he fell through the cracks in the healthcare and justice systems, and wants to know why he turned out to be the way he is.

Juhl says his victims were of no particular "type" and consisted of all hair colors, body sizes, and ages— Mary "Mickey" Fleming was the youngest. The killer refers to himself as an animal.

"He knew right from wrong," says Juhl.

I visit Dad one afternoon when our conversation turns to Mickey. Dad's face reddens, and he starts coughing. Weak from dealing with prostate cancer, he draws his wadded handkerchief from his back pocket, snaps out its wrinkles, and blows his nose into a week's worth of dried nasal residue. I know the routine, and watch him blow each nostril like a trumpet producing that G natural note Mickey and I discovered one day. Then he blows a second time into the mess. If you close your eyes, you can picture a pressure cooker releasing steam. Finally, he swipes the cloth side-to-side across both nostrils. We used to scatter like minnows when Dad pulled out his booger rag.

He leads me to the basement, where he pulls a green plastic box, about the size of a small briefcase, from the top of a dusty shelf.

"Here, take this," he says. "I don't need it any more." He knows the cancer is winning the battle—so he's cleaning house.

The box is crammed with over forty newspaper clippings he cut from the *St. Louis Globe-Democrat*, the *St. Louis Post-Dispatch*, the *St. Charles Journal*, and the *St. Charles edition of the Post*. The articles document the day of Mickey's murder and beyond LaRette's trial and conviction. The headline in the last clipping, dated October 11, 1989, reads "Murderer Will Not Be Extradited." The article focuses on LaRette's confession to the 1978 killing of Tracy J. Miller, a Kansas judge's wife.

I remember how word of that confession spread through my family. The victim's family lives in the St. Louis area, and I wonder if one of us should contact them. Tracy had a sixteen-month-old toddler when LaRette killed her. By the time of the article, that little girl is twelve, and has a new mother. I think about contacting Tracy's family. Maybe I can bring them some further healing, or something—I don't know. The comfort they got from LaRette's capture had come by way of Mickey's death. Do they want to say something to my family too? After thinking about it, I conclude it's too big of a risk. It might bring up too much pain, so I don't try to reach them. As I examine the contents of the box, I know this is information I am supposed to have—reference material that I'll be able to use some day.

Whenever Dad tries to convince anyone that he is telling the truth—or not exactly lying—he places his right hand on his heart, raises his left hand, and says, "Hand to God!" This is short for: "May the Almighty strike me dead if I'm not telling the truth." He claims the Virgin Mary has appeared to him several times. It's never clear to us why this happens. He says the Mother of God never speaks during her brief visits, but her presence always assures him that he'll emerge unharmed from whatever dilemma in which he's found himself embroiled. Every time he talks about these visions, he ends his story with his hand raised toward heaven, swearing they happen. He probably sees her a lot.

Over the years, he built several brick-and-concrete shrines housing two-foot-high white Madonna statues. He had a massive heart attack two weeks after Mom's funeral, while building another shrine—and it nearly killed him. They removed six arteries from his legs and grafted them onto his heart. At the hospital, I asked if he saw the Virgin during the attack. He said she not only appeared to him, she finally spoke to him and told him he'd see her one more time—on his deathbed.

Dad recovers exceptionally well from his sextuple bypass surgery, but prostate cancer kills him in 1992. He outlived Mom by ten years, but unlike Mom, who left a small life insurance policy for us to split, Dad leaves us nothing. Weeks before he died, he had persuaded some of us that we would split a large insurance policy. He left having a good laugh thinking some of us had taken him seriously.

May 10, 1993: Federal District Court denies LaRette's petition for writ of habeas corpus.

March 1, 1994: Federal District Court declines reconsideration of its decision.

January 11, 1995: U.S. Court of Appeals for 8th Circuit affirms District Court decision not to rehear petition for writ of habeas corpus.

March 27, 1995: U.S. Court of Appeals for 8th Circuit denies rehearing.

October 2,1995: U.S. Supreme Court denies LaRette's petition for writ of certiorari.

October 12, 1995: Missouri Supreme Court sets execution date for November 29, 1995.

Potosi Correctional Center, Missouri, November 15, 1995: Pat Juhl makes her seventh and final trip in six years to visit LaRette, the only death row suspect she'd ever investigated. With few exceptions, Juhl had been LaRette's only contact. Several crime authors had failed in their attempts to solicit information from him.

A diligent detective, Juhl had worked days at the Pinellas County Sheriff's Office, and then at home into the night spreading LaRette's and other case files across the dining room table, phoning police departments around the country trying to obtain old reports and crime scene photos. She would exhaust herself from sifting through notes and paperwork and writing reports to be typed later.

Pinellas County had been proactive in unsolved murder cases, but budget constraints put a heavy workload on personnel. Juhl had taken no sick leave during her first four years on the case. On top of everything, her 27-yr-old son, Troy, had been diagnosed with Hodgkin's Disease in October, and she had been visiting him regularly in Ohio.

"The [LaRette] case is always working on her, as far as being on her mind," says her husband, Sgt. Mel Juhl. "Every case she is on, maybe she loses a little of herself. When Pat works on a case, there is no holding her back. She gives it her all."

Juhl's boss, Lt. Gary Herbein, says he can tell by her mood when she receives an upsetting card or letter from LaRette. "It takes a very strong person to do what she has to do," Herbein says.

Through her investigation of Anthony J. LaRette Jr., Juhl is able to close the books on five murders in Florida and ten in other states. She obtains information on fifteen other rapes and murders as well as countless burglaries and assaults.

LaRette believes he murdered 23 to 25 people. He buried two teenage hitchhikers in Florida on an old peacock farm—now Clearwater Mall—where he rode horses in his youth. He beat a woman to death with a claw hammer on the state's Treasure Island, and he claimed to have stomped a woman to death with his heavy boots in Virginia. LaRette claims to have murdered some people whose bodies have never been found, and these cases still remain open.

On Juhl's final visit, LaRette thanks her for shaking hands with him during their first meeting six years earlier and for not seeming repulsed by him. He describes two more murders he'd committed in Fort Myers, Florida. LaRette asks Juhl if she will attend his execution. She declines because she is scheduled to attend a family gathering and visit her son Troy, who has been receiving chemotherapy for lymphoma. "He seems to understand that family comes first," says Juhl. She grants him permission to write to Troy.

As a final request, LaRette asks Juhl if she would scatter his ashes off a pier and into the Gulf of Mexico at Fort DeSoto, Florida. She tells him she will try.

Early in October 1995, I hear a radio news blurb that LaRette's execution by lethal injection has been set. I contact the maximum security prison at Potosi, Missouri, where they are holding him, and ask to witness the execution. They send me an application form that will allow one member of the victim's family to witness the event. I decide to make every effort to be there. He was the last person to be with Mickey while she was alive and conscious, and I'll be there when he dies. Somehow, it completes a circle.

I write two letters to my sister's murderer while he waits in prison. On October 5, 1995, I tell him who I am, and ask him if I can talk to him about a story I'm trying to write about the murder. I want to present him as a person and not a stereotype. Can he remember anything Mickey screamed as he was killing her? I tell him she comes from a large family, who will appreciate anything he can remember. Asking these questions seems insane, but only he knows what happened. I want to know if she called out my name. In those final minutes, did she think of me? Was I in her mind and heart?

Angela Turnbow, a prison representative, discusses my letter with LaRette, and calls me. She says he doesn't want to deal with anything other than his preparations for the execution. He is tired of the life he is living and wants to die.

On October 24, 1995, I write a second letter in which I tell him how I prevented Dad from killing him. I ask him if he wishes I had not intervened. Turnbow calls again and says it is pointless to write, he isn't going to respond.

Sergeant Marsha Baird of the Shawnee County Sheriff's Office in Topeka, Kansas writes to me. Ms. Baird says LaRette's refusal to respond to my letters goes hand-in-hand with his need to depersonalize his victims. To correspond with me will make murdering Mickey too real. "It would have ruined his fantasy of events, which he translates into a loss of control," she writes.

Her description fits right in with LaRette's detached attitude that day on the courthouse steps fifteen years earlier. His shrug had disturbed and insulted me. How could anyone be so indifferent to the murder of another human being? At the time, we didn't know he was a serial killer. I thought Mickey had been his only victim, but he'd had plenty of practice. He didn't understand that it was the most horrible event of our lives. He couldn't have empathized with us. He didn't care.

On November 21, 1995, I receive an official document and a letter telling me to report to the Administration Building at the Potosi Correctional Center on November 28. I am to present the document and my driver's license to the personnel at the facility entrance by 10:30 p.m. Just after midnight, I'll be able to witness the execution. I don't tell anyone, except my wife, Kathy. (After two failed marriages, I've found someone who loved me unconditionally. We have a son named Patrick.)

The next day on my lunch hour, I leave the laboratory and drive toward a nearby park. I wonder about the nature of death. The mobile above Megan's crib and the extraordinary growth of the plant in the Virgin Mary planter could be signs of some kind of afterlife—a different life in a different form. If life continues after the body dies, it makes death the opposite of birth, not the opposite of life. So what is the opposite of life? Is it non-life, non–existence? Will I be witnessing the destruction of LaRette's body, but not the elimination of his existence? Will his spirit be set free, or will it live on to suffer somewhere?

I plan to pick up some lunch and eat at a picnic table in the fresh air and sunlight. While channel surfing on my car radio, I catch a piece of a talk show I listen to occasionally. The topic startles me so much that I nearly run a stoplight. The show's host, Bruce Bradley, is taking calls about the death penalty. When Bradley's passionate about something, his show becomes lively.

Several calls leave little doubt about the host's attitude concerning execution—the sooner we kill them, the better—and from what I'm hearing, his audience is with him. Bradley and his callers are talking about executing people as if it were as easy as putting out the trash, but I'm going to watch a man die in two days. I hear the call-in number, but don't have a cell phone, so I continue to drive, repeating the number until I arrive at an Olive Garden restaurant a mile down the road.

At an indoor pay phone near the entrance of the restaurant, I call Kathy, tell her the station number, and ask her to record the show. I can't believe what is happening—hearing the program so close to LaRette's execution date. After several busy signals, I get the screener and tell her I'm going to witness an execution in a couple of days. She puts me on hold for a few minutes. When I get on the air, I tell Bradley about my initial rage and hatred, and my desire to rip out LaRette's heart, but when I suggest that executing criminals like LaRette might not be the best thing for society, his response is quick.

"Who cares?"

I make a rabies analogy, saying that if scientists had simply killed rabid dogs, they'd never have found an antidote. I say we should consider serial killing a mental illness and search for its possible genetic and environmental influences in order to learn as much as we can about its causes. Otherwise, there is no hope. It will continue to plague us.

"Rabies is a physical disease," Bradley says. "This kind of thinking goes off in wheel-spinning territory. Jeffrey Dahmer's brain is preserved somewhere, so some day they might find a gene. Dahmer killed people and ate them! The problem is that people don't want to accept that there are people who are just evil—immersed in their own evil."

I mention my military experience, and Bruce uses me as an example of a person, trained to kill in service to our country, who later experiences the emotions of hatred and revenge but manages to restrain himself.

"You made a choice, Dennis. These murderers make the wrong choice. It has nothing to do with a quirk in their brain."

I cover one ear and speak loudly over the clanging of dishes and silverware, people talking in the lobby or over lunch, and slamming restroom and kitchen doors. The hostess keeps glancing in my direction, and I worry that she thinks I'm tying up the phone.

"If it were up to me, I'd have them locked away in concrete and studied. I don't believe they're born evil," I say.

"No, I don't either," he says.

"Something in their environment, maybe parental abuse—."

"Maybe it's their fault, Dennis."

"It's their fault, and you're not going to walk out of your house some day and announce that you're pissed off and you're going to kill somebody," I say.

"Neither are you, Dennis, because we're not evil."

"Well, if enough trauma happened to us, we could."

"I'm stunned with this conversation," Bradley says. "I was with you until then. The point that you leave us with is that either you're dead wrong or you're a better man than I am," he says. "Two possibilities might coexist. Maybe you have a better capacity for forgiveness and understanding, but I can't go that far."

160

To make his point about choice, he gives an example of two women who were molested by their fathers. One woman eventually killed her own two children. The second woman became Miss America. This, he says, shows that their decisions have nothing to do with their fathers' abuse. People, he says, can overcome such stuff.

I tell him how I stopped Dad from killing LaRette, and that I believe Dad showed me the razor because subconsciously he wanted me to stop him.

"Telling me your dad showed you the razor as a subconscious plea tells me you're too steeped in psychological study to be salvaged, Dennis. I think you've gone over the edge."

We laugh. It's an opportunity for him to end the call, and he says he hopes the execution helps me in some way.

I get a table and order lunch, feeling good that I've contributed to the public discourse on the topic. I have the impression he doesn't really think I'm dead wrong.

Potosi Correctional Center, November 27, 1995: Anthony J. LaRette Jr. is moved into a 48-hour holding cell and awaits his execution.

On the morning before the execution, I go to work as usual. I don't mention to anybody that I'll be witnessing LaRette's death, and I'm lucky that no one brings it up. People must have heard, and probably leave me alone out of respect. I'm not calm, excited, or nervous when I get home—I'm numb. Someone from a local TV news station calls and wants to come over and talk to me. It's an opportunity to get the Arizona photograph of Mickey on the news. The picture hangs on a wall at the end of our second floor hallway, next to the master bedroom.

A woman reporter and a cameraman show up at about 6 p.m. Kathy and I lead them to the photograph, and they get some footage.

"I hope you can use this photograph," I say. "It's *really* her. Her expression is so much better than the high school photo stations have always shown."

The conversation turns toward why I'm going to witness the execution, and I become emotional. The heat from the camera light is intense, and I'm starting to sweat. The reporter asks how I feel about watching LaRette die.

"Turn it off," I say, directing my comment to the cameraman.

She says viewers will understand my emotions, and they will understand the significance of my loss. Many will remember the coverage fifteen years earlier. My face reddens, and the base of my throat tightens.

"I can't do that," I say.

Kathy puts an arm around me.

"They want a sound bite, Denny. You should let people see what Mickey meant to you."

"She's not a sound bite. All they'll see is me getting upset," I say.

I escort them to the front door, say I hope they'll use the picture, and then go upstairs and put on a jacket and tie. After all, it's a kind of funeral, and I want to represent the family well.

Potosi is a small Midwestern town about an hour's drive southwest of St. Louis, down Missouri Highway 21 in the rolling foothills of the Ozark Mountains. A couple of factories and the YMCA are its large employers. Nevertheless, an ugly elephant sits about two miles east of town on 140 acres off Highway O near the intersection of Missouri 21 and Highway 8. The Potosi Correctional Center (the PCC) houses about 800 male inmates, maximum security and high-risk individuals—and those sentenced to death. All executions in Missouri take place in the facility.

Around 9:30 p.m., I pull into a small gas station and convenience store just a few miles from Potosi, and pick up a pack of cigarettes. There's a burning sensation high in my stomach, as if I've swallowed a habanero pepper. A shot of whiskey chased with a beer will kill it, but I don't want my perceptions of the execution altered —and I don't want the smell of the family weakness on my breath.

Dr. Dalbey and I had discussed my nervous cigarette cravings. I sometimes want a cigarette, even though I quit nearly fifteen years earlier and have run thousands of miles. "Look at it this way. It's better than drinking or taking drugs. You smoke a pack of cigarettes, then stop. Big deal," he'd said.

I turn onto Highway 8, drive about a mile, and then take Highway O to the PCC. It's early, so I pass by it. There's nothing remarkable about the building—concrete with the standard razor wire in whorls across the top of the walls.

I passed a McDonald's restaurant near the intersection of Highways 21 and 8. Feeling hollow and light headed, I drive back there, and reluctantly enter the restaurant. Never having watched a man put to death, I don't know what to expect. I might throw up anything I eat. Yet, the familiar odor of hamburgers and fries makes me hungry.

Generic '70s disco music plays on an oldies radio station. The only patrons besides me are two men in their forties sitting near a window to the right of the entrance. A thin woman with coal dark hair in a ponytail smiles at me from behind the counter and takes my order. I fill a soda cup at the machine, and sit at a small table under music bubbling from a ceiling speaker. A news blurb interrupts. It's about LaRette's execution.

I'm staring at the speaker in the white ceiling, when I become aware that the other two customers are debating who is wearing the uglier tie. One of them signals to the woman behind the counter.

"Hey, Miss. Excuse me, but we need an unbiased opinion." He raises the lower part of his tie with the back of his hand, and his friend raises his in competition. She can clearly see the patterns on the ties—neither of which I'd be caught dead in.

"What do you think?" the man asks. "I mean, my tie is pretty bad, but it's respectable next to this guy's. Am I right?"

She leans across the counter to get a better look at them.

"Neither one of you could be married. A woman would never let you leave the house wearing those things. Do they come with a volume control?" They all laugh— and I laugh with them. It feels good to see people enjoying just being with each other, and some of my tension slips away.

"Could you turn them down a notch?" she asks. Then she points at me. "Now there's a man who knows a good tie."

"Thank you. My son gave this to me for Christmas," I say.

"Well, he's got very good taste," she said.

I have on the tie my son Patrick bought for me at the St. Louis Art Museum gift shop, and it features a reproduction of Van Gogh's only unsigned painting, *Café Terrace at Night*. According to historians, Van Gogh painted the picture one day and then offered it to the café proprietor in exchange for a meal. The man felt sorry for the artist and fed him, but he didn't like the painting, so he asked Van Gogh not to bother to sign it.

In the painting, a soft yellow light from the outdoor café spreads out onto the cobblestone street and fades into the deep blue evening sky, speckled with Van Gogh's signature starbursts. I've never thought much about that light before, but tonight it reminds me of the yellow gas station lights I saw during my all-night rides with my brother-in-law on the evening of Mickey's death.

The two men are staring at me, so I raise the tie to let them see it better.

"Is your last name Fleming?" one of them asks. It's Plummer and Harvey—fifteen years older, but still a team. Like myself, they've put on a few pounds. Plummer still has a head of tightly curled hair, and Harvey's formerly dark bushy beard is now trim.

As I walk over to their booth, they stand and we shake hands.

"I never really had the chance to thank you in person," I say.

"We were just doing our job," Plummer says.

"You're here for the execution, right?" asks Harvey.

"Yeah," I say.

"You can follow us over there, if you'd like," says Plummer.

166

"I'd like that," I say.

We talk about my family, with people scattered around the country and Mom and Dad dead. Then they tell me how they managed to get LaRette out of Kansas, a state with no death penalty, and into Missouri.

They'd listened to LaRette admit that he'd killed Mickey and then immediately launch into his hitchhiker story. They also knew that LaRette was a prime suspect in the 1978 Tracy Miller murder at that time—and that LaRette had been arraigned years earlier in Judge Miller's court for other charges, which meant the judge knew who he was. But Harvey and Plummer had worked hard to gain custody of LaRette, and they didn't want to lose him. So somehow, without breaking any laws, they managed to leave the Topeka police station with LaRette and drive toward St. Charles. Traffic slowed as they approached the Kansas-Missouri state line, and they could see the familiar flashing lights of cop cars, so Plummer and Harvey started to worry. They figured the judge had used his influence—pulling whatever strings judges pull, to make sure LaRette stayed in Kansas. However, when they approached the police dragnet, they realized it was a random sobriety check. They flashed their credentials and crossed the state line, where the judge no longer had the pull to stop them.

I follow Plummer's car to the PCC and turn into the driveway past a group of demonstrators. Most are anti-death penalty advocates, but a few signs say things like: "An eye for an eye."

Plummer and Harvey check in ahead of me at the guard station. I drive up to the guard and hand him my driver's license and the papers I received from the state. He tells me where to park, but I just follow Plummer and Harvey about a hundred feet into a surprisingly large paved lot where I park under a light post next to their plain, unmarked police car. Again, a faint trace of ominous gas station light lies over the asphalt.

Without a word, we walk toward the building, and I look up at the stars, clearly visible in the cloudless autumn night sky—a Van Gogh sky. The silence is making me nervous. "I guess this is nothing new to you guys."

"This is the first time for both of us, and I don't plan on any others," says Harvey.

"Me, neither," says Plummer. "We've kept track of this animal from the beginning—any time he did anything. Motion for a new trial, certiorari at the U.S. Supreme Court, post-conviction relief, writ of habeas corpus, you name it. Fifteen years. We're following this to the end."

"Do you know if his parents are going to be here?" I ask.

Harvey shakes his head and looks at the Van Gogh sky.

"Those crazies couldn't get within a mile of here."

"I know his father tried to break him out of jail, but what about his mother?" I ask.

"She's nuttier than the old man," Plummer says.

An official meets us at the door and escorts us through a series of metal detectors, locked hatches, and barred doors. It's white and bright inside as if I have finally stepped into the source of the strange gas station light. We have to remove everything—change, wallets, wristwatches, belts, shoes, and my Van Gogh tie—keeping on only our shirts, pants, socks, and shoes.

Somewhere during the process, I find myself seated at a low gray table in a small nondescript room. A heavyset woman sitting at the other end of the table leans forward. "This is yours to keep," she says, gently placing her right-hand fingertips on a green pocket folder and sliding it over to me.

The folder contains an execution packet for the news media, a brief description of LaRette's criminal activities, and two recent photographs of him. The pictures are tightly cropped, medium close-ups, one in which he faces the camera and the other a profile facing left. In both shots, he is holding a black Department of Corrections identification plaque—one of those reusable slates with white plastic letters imbedded in horizontal felt furrows. He is identified as ANTHONY LARETTE, CP 12. (All 90 male death row inmates were designated CP. There were three women on death row at the time. They were designated CPF.)

"My job is to make sure you understand what you are about to observe this evening," says the woman, in an unexpectedly soft voice. "The pictures in the folder were taken recently."

I figure this is going to be some kind of test of my intent or self-control.

"This is the man as he looks today. You are going to witness the state of Missouri take *this man's* life. I'm here to draw your attention to this, give you a moment to reflect. If you'd like to reconsider, now's the time."

The man in the photos doesn't look much like the LaRette I remember. His face is expressionless, his eyes dull and staring into nowhere. He's wearing a white T-shirt. His hair is straight, oily, and thinning, and he's balding in front. It has grown long enough in the back to drape over a collar, were he wearing one. A thin, braided extension of hair about six inches long—one small sign of individuality and rebellion—runs between his shoulder blades. He's gained weight, probably from the prison food, and his neck is thick.

"I'm not here so much to watch him die. I need to be here *when* he dies," I say. "I owe that to my sister."

A guard accompanies me out of the room, and leads me down a long hallway to an immense, thick metal door. Once on the other side, I stand in a short section of the hall, and wait until an identical door at the other end opens. Once I step through that door, the world, as the inmates call it, is gone, and I feel like a prisoner. A lockdown is in effect. All inmates are locked in their cells. I imagine the usual background sound of hundreds of inmates, talking, and yelling, some even laughing, which only deepens the silence.

I enter a room in which Harvey and Plummer have joined a small group that has gathered. We sign something like a logbook for witnesses, before the guards usher us into a miniature theater of sorts, three rows of five seats. I take a front-row chair directly in front of the only window in the room. Intuition, and the looks I receive from the other attendees, tells me they know I'm a family member. It's my right to sit up front and center, and I don't think anyone disagrees.

The window's horizontal blinds are closed, and I wonder what I will see when they open. Will someone be standing there like a master of ceremonies? Will they say something, a statistical summary of LaRette's life of crime? Will they mention his rape conviction in Lawrence, Kansas, in 1971, for which he received a five- to twenty-year sentence—and served the minimum five? Will they tell us that, in August 1978, he received a one- to ten-year sentence for something he'd done in Topeka —but he served only a short time in a county jail? Had he served even two years of that sentence, he wouldn't have been in St. Charles to murder Mickey. I wouldn't be sitting here, now.

Some of those present wear press badges. Several officials quietly stand as sentries about ten feet to my left.

No one speaks, as if we are attending a church service and waiting for the minister to arrive. "I'm here for you, Mickey" keeps running through my mind.

The blinds open more slowly than I expected them to. LaRette lies covered with a white sheet and strapped in a hospital bed. The head of the bed is against a far wall in the otherwise empty white room. Tubes run from the wall to the bed, under the sheets and into his left arm. He stares across the room and away from me, toward a window to his right, through which I see a man and a woman standing. Their eyes are fixed upon him. I learn later that the man, a Dr. Brede, is the chairman of the criminal justice department at Kansas State University. He is one of the few people who interviewed LaRette more than once. The woman is Sergeant Marsha Baird of Shawnee County Sheriff's Department, Topeka, Kansas.

A voice comes over an intercom, announcing they are about to execute LaRette, why, and how—three chemical injections and the purpose of each. As the first injection, a tranquilizer, goes into him, LaRette calmly mouths the words "I'm okay" to Dr. Brede, and then closes his eyes as if going to sleep. This first injection is crucial. If it's improperly administered, LaRette might experience the pain of the subsequent drugs that will eventually kill him.

The second injection hits him, and he stops breathing and arches his body. His eyes briefly spring wide open, and he stares at the ceiling. What does he see? His chest swells as his lungs strain for breath, and his stomach muscles ripple unnaturally. I think he is going to vomit, but then he goes limp.

The sheet covering him quivers, almost imperceptibly, until the third injection finally stops his heart from beating. A few moments later, the voice from the intercom pronounces LaRette dead. Officials standing to my left could easily be standing at a funeral, which I suppose it is, in a strange sort of way. The state has taken a life, and out of respect for all life, they have accomplished the task quietly, honorably.

Anthony Joe LaRette Jr. dies at 12:12 a.m.

Any man facing imminent death and given the opportunity to make a final statement probably rehearses his words, to be clear so they come out correctly. LaRette's final statement reads: "To my family and loved ones, I love them and I'm sorry it had to come this way."

He's sorry his death has to come "*this way*," as an execution for murder, as if his death should come some other way. Of course it should. Who, other than someone with a painful terminal disease, would want to die by lethal injection?

Had LaRette meant to say that he's sorry his *life* resulted in an execution? It would have been an apology for becoming a killer and a rapist, but that isn't what he said. His statement focuses on his *death*, not his life. Even during his last moments on Earth, did he continue to disown what he'd done?

The entire world seems upside down. I just watched the execution of a murderer—a man who raped some of his victims after they were dead. In the eyes of many people, he deserved to die. His death has been carried out in a well-lit, peaceful, solemn, antiseptic environment. I understand the state's position not to stoop to the brutality of an individual they execute, but rather rise above it, and treat any life, including LaRette's, with dignity. On the other hand, Mickey, an innocent young woman, just out of high school, with a job and a future, died brutally and bloodily, and the horror of it had been senseless and pointless. I simply can't wrap my mind around these two realities.

They caught LaRette lying throughout the trial, but only he and Mickey knew the truth—and certain things that never came out during the proceedings threatened to drive me mad. *Had I been on her mind and in her heart during her last moments? Had I been deserving of that?* I recalled something the doctor had told me in the emergency room that horrible day. He said that he'd cut open her rib cage on the slim chance that he might save her. Then someone had added, "Perhaps it's better. She was too long without oxygen." At the time, I would have taken Mickey brain dead. I would have taken her any way I could get her, but I've come to realize they were probably right.

A *Post-Dispatch* reporter speaks with me as I leave the PCC. Quotes from Brian, Susie, investigators, and police appear in the evening papers. Hours before the execution, Susie says, "I don't think he'll ever be able to redeem himself. He's caused too much pain for too many people. I'm thanking God that finally he's getting his punishment." Brian adds, "He's hurt too many people. Victims and their family members. Every night, every day, I think about Mary. I've been waiting for (the execution) ever since this man…killed my baby sister. I've been waiting for him to sweat blood. I don't mean to sound so bad, but this is long overdue."

I wish I could gain something from the execution —catharsis or closure—but I don't. LaRette's death only satisfies my need to be there when it happens, because he was there when Mickey died. I'm depressed. It's the only feeling I have—a deep sadness fills me.

Detective Pat Juhl from Florida is quoted in the *Post-Dispatch* as saying, "Just three weeks ago he had offered clues about several murders in Florida." Richard Lee adds, "He cried when he confessed. He'd relive (the crimes) as a way to clean out his conscience. He was very concerned about his salvation." Lee says that investigators used LaRette's Catholic guilt "as a tool to provide us with information." LaRette must have thought he could square his account with God. He didn't ask for a priest to provide him with his last rites. A prison spokesperson,

175

Tim Kniest, is quoted as saying, "His manner was cool. He chatted with prison (officials) up until the execution."

When I tried to contact LaRette, a prison representative told me that he was tired of death row and wanted to die. So what kind of punishment did we ultimately give him? Which is more punishing—fourteen years on death row or death? The article carries a short description of my presence at the execution: "Dennis Fleming, the brother of a LaRette victim, watched the execution as one of the state's seven witnesses. He gave the following account: Inside a dim, drab room, LaRette lay on a gurney with a white sheet covering him up to his neck. His face was pale, his mood calm. He turned his head to [a⊠ female acquaintance and, in exaggerated syllables, mouthed, 'I'm okay.' It was over. He was dead, and I felt an overall sense of sadness for the state of humankind. I believe justice was done, but I don't know if I can ever forgive him. Maybe God will grant him salvation. Maybe." I must have been unclear about to whom LaRette directed his final words, or the reporter got it wrong. They say I cried—but I don't remember.

"LaRette refused to take sedatives before the start of the lethal injection sequence. He wanted to be in control all during the entire procedure. In control—those two words sum up the way Tony committed his crimes and the manner in which he confessed to them. The descriptions he gave were always about what he'd done and the manner in

which he depersonalized the victim."—Sgt. Marsha Baird, Shawnee County Sheriff's Office, Topeka, Kansas

The Register-Guard, Eugene, Oregon, Sunday, December 10, 1995: "To a certain degree, he used me and I used him. All his murders were very detailed. I'm sure he relived them a lot when he was there in prison. My whole attitude with him was it's worth it if I can solve the crimes or help resolve the families' emotions. He considered me a friend. He wasn't my friend. But...I do respect the man for giving up what information he did. Because he could have went (sic) to his execution never opening his mouth."— Pinellas County Detective Pat Juhl

The Gainesville Sun, Sunday, December 10, 1995: "To me, it was so unbelievable that he could do all of these things for all these years and not get caught. He needed a friend. I needed information. I got to know him as Tony LaRette on death row. I got to know him as a human being. I would dump [the ashes] for him. Basically what it amounted to at the time was, I didn't want to say, 'I won't do that. I don't want your ashes.' Because I was there to get information. If a container showed up some day, I guess I'd look at it as I'll do this because of the information he did provide. LaRette ended up being my career. It's like a closing in part of my career. Maybe I'll delve into LaRette's unsolved cases again. Some day. It's my own curiosity. I'd like to know." —Pinellas County Detective Pat Juhl

Four months after LaRette's execution, Juhl decides to put a close to her association with the killer. She makes a call to his attorney and inquires whether LaRette's ashes had been sent to a family member. She discovers his body is still in the morgue with a request that, following cremation, the ashes be sent to her.

Pinellas County Sheriff's Office, Largo, Florida, Spring 1996: A package containing LaRette's ashes addressed to Detective Juhl arrives at the Pinellas County police station. Juhl drives to Fort DeSoto, Florida, and scatters his ashes into the Gulf of Mexico. "I believe in an afterlife, and I don't want to run into Tony and have him ask me why I didn't scatter his ashes," says Juhl.

Pinellas County, Florida, Wednesday, May 29, 1996: For her six-year investigation of serial killer Anthony J. LaRette Jr., Detective Pat Juhl is honored. Juhl receives the prestigious Ruth and Tim Johnson Law Enforcement Detective of the Year Award for 1995 and the Medal of Valor from the National Sheriffs' Association. Through dedication and perseverance, Detective Juhl was able to close cases in Florida—including the Pinellas County murders of Betty H. Brunton in 1976 and Helen Alderson Hall in 1978—and similar rape and murder cases in five other states. The Clearwater Kiwanis Club presents Juhl with a check for $1,000.

Part IV
Deliverance

The aim of art is to represent not the outward appearance of things, but their inward significance.
—Aristotle

Now and then, I'm talking with someone at a screenwriting workshop or writing seminar, and the issue of loss and its dramatic elements pops up. I mention how I lost Mickey, and the universal response is that I should write a screenplay about it. Although I want to do something artistic to honor Mickey, I don't want to exploit her death. I once developed a rough dramatic storyline, but then felt ashamed I'd fictionalized my sister's death into melodrama, and abandoned the project.

But a nebulous *Mickey story* won't let go of me, until I meet Diana Ossana at the Austin Heart of Film Screenwriters Conference in Texas. Diana, an accomplished novelist and screenwriter, suggests I write a nonfiction book, not a screenplay, about Mickey. It never occurred to me to write a personal story about my special relationship with Mickey, the impact her death had on me, and the hope I took away from it. I simply never thought to pour out my thoughts and emotions. No one ever suggested I write a memoir. The idea is liberating.

I nearly burst into tears, rush back to my room, open a spiral bound notebook, and start writing—at last free to record my feelings, uninhibited and unhindered. I'm released from the constraints of the screenplay dramatic structure and my concern that I might do disservice to Mickey. In fact, I'm doing something wonderful for her, and I laugh at the irony of having to attend a screenwriting conference in order to discover a passion for writing a nonfiction book.

Driving back to St. Louis, I'm high with an excitement that feels as if it will never end.

After nearly a year writing about Mickey every day, I begin to wonder if I've been kidding myself. Has Mickey, and the manner of her death, really had a significant, positive impact on me, or am I still obsessing over her because I haven't truly come to terms with the emotional trauma of her death? Have I blown my relationship with her out of proportion? I spent far less time with Mickey than with my other siblings. Am I fooling myself? I begin writing fiction and poetry and essays based on other events in my life. Yet, every day, something reminds me of Mickey. I see a young girl who looks like her, a song brings her to mind, or sometimes she just pops into my mind for no reason.

Although I can't get through a day without thinking about Mickey, I set aside the idea of honoring her artistically—until the day I find a small used book titled *Brancusi vs. United States* in a museum bookstore. Any Brancusi work brings Mickey to my mind because of its association with the Virgin Mary planter Mom gave me. When I get home, I read the book and discover it isn't a biography or a conversation about Brancusi's *oeuvre*—it's a court transcript.

In 1928, Constantin Brancusi brought a case against the U.S. government to determine the definition of art. In the end, his sculpture *Bird in Space*—the example of his work upon which the judge rendered his decision—was declared a work of art principally because it served no utilitarian purpose and was purely ornamental. The court deemed the piece beautiful, symmetrical, pleasing to look at, and exemplifying a new school of art that attempted to represent abstract ideas rather than true objects.

I contemplate writing a screenplay based on the case. I'll have to research the full background to find a storyline, and though the case fascinates me, I question how I can dramatize it. The story inspires me to enroll in an adult evening class in stone sculpting.

I'm trying to come up with an idea for a screenplay based on the Brancusi case while strolling on a path behind our apartments along a wooded area separating fifty yards of dense brush and tall trees from a shallow creek. I pass by a familiar trail that leads to an old abandoned tree house Patrick discovered a year earlier, when he was ten. We had several tree house chats there, and each time, upon our return to the main path, I notice the same piece of unfinished concrete protruding out of dense tangled weeds and decaying tree limbs just off the trail. Today, for no particular reason I can think of, other than it might be a piece of sculpture, I decide to find out exactly what the structure is.

The first two things I notice don't seem extraordinary. The section of concrete I can clearly see is two inches by two inches square and a couple of feet long. It looks like the leg of a primitive concrete chair. A flat piece of rusted iron, about an inch wide and four inches long, sticks out from the bottom of the structure. I can see three dime-sized holes in the metal—possibly for attaching the object to something.

I step off the path and clear away some weeds so I can see the thing better. Part of it extends out perpendicularly from the main leg section. I get a grip where the two pieces intersect and pull upward, taking care not to strain my problem back. After several minutes of moving it a few inches at a tug, I'm able to pull it out of the weeds. As I drag it onto the main path, I realize that it is a large heavy cross made from low grade concrete. The rusty metal piece is on the bottom and is probably used to attach the cross to another structure. I stand it upright and hold it steady. It's about three and a half feet tall and weighs about eighty pounds. I think of the Brancusi trial. "This thing is not art. It has utility." I turn it around to see an arrangement of pea-sized, asymmetric white stones that form letters set into the concrete at half-inch intervals. It is a crude way to inscribe a grave marker.

The letters R.I.P. run down the vertical section above the horizontal, and a large zero or letter O made with stones is on the bottom vertical. Someone has gone to a lot of trouble. Has it been made for a pet dog or cat? Does a zero mean that the puppy or kitten died before its first birthday?

I read the large letters, formed with little stones across the horizontal section of the cross, and I shudder—they spell *Mickey*.

I sit on the path, and look at the cross for a long time.

When I get home, Kathy reminds me that it's Good Friday, and *this* puts a spin on everything. The cross isn't technically a crucifix, because it has no effigy of Jesus attached to it. Yet used as a grave marker, I think most people would call it a Christian symbol. Brancusi's art connected me with the Virgin Mary planter, and now, in a strange way, it connects me to the cross. The psychiatrist Carl Jung believed that highly improbable coincidences that have powerful connections to significant things or events probably aren't accidents. At least, that's the theory.

Though not a practicing Christian, I can relate to the symbolism of a buried cross I find on Good Friday, the celebration of the release of Christ's spirit, after much physical pain and suffering, which points to eternal life. The unexplained growth of the plant in the Virgin planter following Mom's death suggests the release of Mom's spirit and its union with Mickey—life after life—just as Mom had told me. What am I supposed to learn from these Christian signs of an afterlife associated with Mickey? What about the *zero or letter* O? What does that mean?

Back when the family learned that Dad had contacted one of his friends to make Mickey's headstone, we all were afraid that he was going to produce something cheap and embarrassing. We thought he should have talked with us first. However, Dad surprised everyone by having a simple and attractive gray stone installed—but it contains a major flaw. Mickey had died in 1980, but the headstone reads *1981*. We can understand getting Mickey's birthday wrong, but the year she died was current when the stonecutter stamped the date. Dad's stone carver, we determine, was probably drunk or stoned when he chiseled the wrong date. It's something that has always bothered me, and no one in the family has changed it yet.

I've been chiseling limestone in sculpting class, so I resolve to try changing the *one* on Mickey's headstone to a *zero*. On a hot June afternoon, I set out for Mickey's grave in St. Charles. Visiting her grave is always like stepping back in time to the burial day. Faint images of people move about in my head, and I keep looking at the spot where Mom had been sitting in the car crying. In my mind, Mickey's casket still hangs suspended above the grave, a single red rose lying in the middle of a blood smear, my blood running down the side of the box, the specter of LaRette lurking on the periphery.

Mickey's headstone is about two feet tall, too short for me to carve on its front, so I tip it over and start cutting on the erroneous number *one* in the '81. It only takes a few strikes before I know I'm ruining it. The stone is just too dense for my tools. I'll have to take the next step in my mysterious journey of symbols. The Virgin Mary planter, the Brancusi, and the cross have led me back to where it all began—Mickey's grave—and I'll have to buy a new headstone and see what happens next.

I keep the cross and the planter in my office next to a decapitated Madonna statue I found lying on Mickey's grave fifteen years ago. It's probably one of Dad's statues, so I've kept the head and body all these years, but I've never reattached them and sanded and repainted it. Out of some kind of respect for Dad, I've left it alone, and maybe we all left the headstone alone for the same reason. In his own way, he tried to honor his daughter. But it's time to fix things. So, I reattach the head with gray resin that leaves a dark necklace around the Virgin's neck. I set it on the floor near the window to dry.

A few months later, Kathy sees it and asks me when I'm going to paint it and hide the gray ring around its neck. She says it's eerie and reminds her of how Mickey's throat was sliced. I sand it and paint it white, and then set it next to Mickey's headstone at the cemetery.

It's summer. I'm recovering from a sinus cold and staring at the computer monitor trying to come up with a short piece of writing. Events from my past keep creeping in: a hermit who lived in his hand-built concrete fortress a few miles from our house when we were kids; Dad's failed attempt to drive across a flooded road; and the time he crashed into the back of the drive-in movie screen during the movie *Samson and Delilah*. Memories are swirling around in my head and not letting me concentrate. I glance at the concrete cross. *When am I going to write about Mickey and how her death changed my life? What about the signs, the meaningful coincidences?* I have to do something, I have to get past it, so I try to write it out of me. If it's garbage, it's garbage—but I have to try to get it outside of me.

I call up a blank screen, and write: "Nearly every day I think of my sister, Mickey. She's been eighteen years old for more than twenty-five years now." I write until my neck hurts, and then I stick a note on the lower left side of my computer monitor. It reads:

"It's about Mickey's death, how it affected me, how it affects me now."

Nine months later, around noon on a hot, humid midsummer day, with my first draft—some 64,000 words —finished, I've written so much *about* Mickey that I need to write *to* her. I'm convinced she's still around—somewhere. So I write the words "Dear Mickey," and instantly find myself emotionally back at the gravesite the day we buried her—the day I cried like a baby in Mom's lap.

I have to leave the keyboard because I'm using the shirttail of my white short-sleeved shirt as a handkerchief, and it is soaked. I'm afraid I'll damage the keyboard, so I grab a spiral notebook and go downstairs and sit in the sweltering heat on the steps just outside the basement's back door, and I finish my letter.

I let my deep love for her grow and rise to the surface, pure and natural like sunlight warming the chill off a cold valley. Over the years, I have obscured loss and stifled hateful emotions, burying them under infatuation for women. Grief resurfaced as a misdirected depression when each relationship fell apart. After almost two years of therapy, I realize I hadn't effectively dealt with my grief. Still, I avoid facing the core problem. Instead of working through the grief, I focus on my creativity.

But my promise to Mickey ultimately helps me become whole. It helps me reconnect with the child in me, the creative part of me. Grief has been pulling at me, crying for release. It has taken more than a quarter of a century to work its way out. And release from it finally comes with a letter—more than twenty-five years in the making.

Dear Mickey,

Your death shows me that something exists beyond my life. A consciousness. Something somehow gave me signs. I don't know if what I received was from you and Mom and Dad or some *other*, perhaps God, but there's *something*, and it's a wonderful thing to know it's there.

If you're there when this body of mine dies, I'll find you, even if there is no bright light to go to, even if it's dark. Jump into my arms, Mickey. I won't ask if it's you. I'll just hold you. If I need light, I'll find it, and I'll look at your neck and hands and see them uncut, unscarred—hands that drew butterflies, trees, and sugarplums for me. Hands that wrote *Mary Michelle Fleming* in cursive, practicing, like we all do, variations until you made it your own special signature—one you didn't get to use for long. I'll hold you, stroke your long hair, and tell you I love you, though I don't have to tell you—you know.

Maybe that's how it is. We see people the way we saw them in love. I'll be with Mom, sitting on her lap as she sings and makes me feel special by showing me how, even at five, I could draw better than she could draw.

Dad will be lying with his arms outstretched on the living room floor. I'll try to reach into his open hand, touch his palm, and pull away before his iron claw grabs me, drags me into his embrace, and tickles me.

I'll ride the two-lane highway between St. Charles and Washington with Mike. He'll pull the car over and let me drive. I'll steer the monster-sized Ford on the tiny ribbon of road, excited as I've ever been, with my big brother there to guide me and watch over me.

I'll open a shoebox and pull out a pair of Hush Puppies, a gift from Uncle Bud, shoes I'd forgotten that I'd told him I wanted—but they're the wrong kind. They have laces. They're not slip-ons, and they have black soles instead of tan, gummy ones. They're the wrong shape, too —long and not rounded. I'll put them on and decide that they really don't look bad. I didn't ask for them, but he sent me a pair—and I know he loves me.

I'll meet everyone in love that way.

Maybe I'll see your eyes again, big and blue, looking up at me from your impish smile. I'll make you laugh, and I'll be happy just watching you. You'll tell me I didn't have to think of you so often because you knew I'd see you here.

You'll explain all the signs and why I received them. I rejoice thinking about it, and I'm crying, each tear a sentence or a paragraph. Evidence of my love. You've given me so much to believe in. I'm not afraid to die, but I'm still sad, knowing you died afraid and in pain. I'll always carry that sadness.

If I could change things, I would have stopped by that day to tell you I had the money to help you buy a car. We would have gone to lunch. You would have told me that you'd talked to Dad and that he was giving you some money, too. LaRette would have had to go somewhere else. But he would have continued to hurt others. He would have killed again. Your death gave life to his future victims, countless unknown women who are alive now because *you* tried so hard to live. Now I live with the knowledge of something greater, and it gives me hope for my children and grandchild, for my wife—for everyone.

Thank you, Mickey. I don't think that, during all the years of thinking about you nearly every day, I ever thanked you. How about that—your big brother thanking *you*?

Give my love to Mom, Dad, and Mike, and tell Uncle Bud that I'm going to ask about his adventures with Uncle Ed. I want to know more about those stories and about Francis and the house in Springfield, Illinois. He'll know what I mean. Maybe Ed and Francis have different versions of those stories.

I want to show you some of the things I've learned on Kathy's piano—three blues chords that I play, though not well, endlessly with subtle variations. Kathy always plays right after me to get the bad taste out of her ears. If I have the time, I'll learn a lot more.

I thought about asking you to play "Heart and Soul" with me, but I don't think we'll be able to fit it in. There will be so much to do, so many people to see, so much love to share. It'll be my lifetime. It'll be the drop of a tear.

Love always,
Denny

Almost a week passes. I haven't thought about Mickey, and when she does pop into my mind, I don't feel guilty for not thinking about her.

The following week, I write another letter.

To Anthony Joe LaRette Jr.:

Many police officers called you Tony, but I can't do that. It's too personal. It sounds innocent. I read that your father asked the courts to spell his name LeRette, which was the correct way. It pleases me—I can't tell you why—to know that you died with your name misspelled. Mary Michelle Fleming was my sister. We called her Mickey. Mickey's death gave me evidence of an existence beyond this one.

I was in a discussion about that recently, and someone said, "You know, crazy people talk about spirits and other worlds all the time." It didn't shake my understanding of those things. I didn't see ghosts or spirits, and I had no automatic handwriting messages or tarot card readings. I didn't seek the signs I received. They simply crossed my path and I took notice. I'm telling you this because I'm making an assumption. If Mickey, Mom, Dad, Mike, or any of my deceased family had anything to do with the signs, there's a chance that they can hear me in my heart and my soul. If they're in some other place, perhaps you're also somewhere, and you'll hear what I have to say to you.

Someone once asked if I'd ever forgiven you, and I had to say I didn't know. Knowing your history of mental disorder, the seizures, the blackouts, and your head injuries, I blame our judicial and mental institutions for letting you (and other people like you) remain among the public. I know our internal biology can alter our perception of reality. I was reaching an altered state that I didn't understand as I approached a manic episode in 1992.

Fortunately, I had a boss who believed me when I told him I didn't understand what was happening to me. He thought I'd been snorting cocaine. Some of my coworkers had been complaining about my erratic behavior, of which I was unaware.

My wife, Kathy, encouraged me to see a psychiatrist. My boss insisted I go, or I'd lose my job. My knowledge of pharmaceuticals and experience with therapy led me to think that something had tilted the balance of my brain's chemistry. Kathy took me to a psychiatric health care facility where a psychiatrist, the facility director, told me I probably had bipolar disorder. It's probably genetic. My crazy Uncle Ed was *off the beam*, according to Uncle Bud. They put Uncle Ed in the Nuthouse—the Booby Hatch. He probably was bipolar, too, but that was in the early Fifties, and they treated him with less sophisticated medications. Medications have kept me in balance, and I can sense things change when I run out. I get nerve flushes above my chest. Colors and light vibrate with a brilliant sheen. The meds work, and I'm grateful for them.

Because of you, Anthony, I researched serial killers and pedophiles. I've often thought about how a child abuser steals the emotional and mental life from a child. Emotional destruction is never healed completely, no matter how much therapy they receive. They just have to cope.

I sometimes think about how your father tried to break you out of jail and about your plot to murder police officers and others you felt deserved it. I recall what Officer Plummer or Harvey said the night of your execution. He said your parents wouldn't be there to help you die because they were as crazy as you were. Everything I've read about serial killers tells me that your parents had a hand in making you the monster you became.

You took someone very special from me—and you made her last moments of life the most horrible imaginable. You took Mickey from my family and from her close friends, kids who didn't need to see life's horrors up close. I can never forgive you for that.

If it were up to me, Anthony, you would have sat in jail for the rest of your life, disclosing more information about other women you had raped and murdered. You and murderers like you would be subjects of intense study. We'd discover more about the causes of your behavior and would eventually stop you from being created—because I believe you were created. Your environment and your brain chemistry were out of balance, and we have to learn how to restore that balance. The cost of inaction is too great.

If we continue to kill our problems, we'll watch as children are destroyed, and we will see them turn into killers. They will become like you, a monster walking sick and dangerous among us.

I can't forgive that monster. However, I can have compassion for the child you once were. I can even love that little child—a child who probably took pride in sharing his father's name. In a way, I can feel sorry for you because we all carry, inside us, the child we were. Geniuses from Picasso to Einstein have told us that creativity comes from letting the child within us play—but that inner child has to be healthy.

I can't imagine we have the ability to destroy a soul. But if a soul, even one with a tortured mind, must pay for crimes of the flesh, then I trust you've paid. I can only hope that wherever you are, some kind of balance has been restored.

Dennis Patrick Fleming

Post Script

Detective Pat Juhl believes that things are interconnected, and we are wise to pay attention to coincidences that appear meaningful. While investigating the LaRette case, Pat collected ceramic pigs and pig memorabilia. She and her husband were cops, i.e. "pigs," and her father worked on a pig farm. Some time after LaRette's death, Pat discontinued her pig collection and impulsively began collecting Virgin Mary planters. She collects them to this day, and marveled at the coincidence in my planter story when she met me. To honor that coincidence, I tried to give Pat the planter Mom had given me, but Pat told me to keep it, because it connected me to Mom and Mickey. Pat's a strong woman, and her story is heroic. It's been an honor to talk with her.

When my brother, Mark, read the first edition of this book, he was concerned about only one section of it: Did I really find the cross on Good Friday, and did it have Mickey's name on it? I said, "Yes," and he asked what I thought it meant. I said it had something to do with Mickey in the afterlife, and I needed to change the one to a zero on the tombstone. He said that was true, but it was also a message for me to get right with Jesus. I said he might be right, but I didn't think much about it.

On April 8, 2010, Mark died of a heart attack. He was 58. At the time, I was rewriting this new edition of the book you are reading, and working on the section where I find the cross, take it home, and try to rationalize its significance in relation to the growth of the lily in the Madonna planter. I was thinking about the Brancusi connection, the spinning toy above Megan's bed, and Pat Juhl's decision to collect Madonna planters and how LaRette's attempt at Catholic redemption related to that.

As I said, I got the word Mark died moments after he had passed away at the exact moment I was rewriting the section, and intensely pondering what meaning the cross might have. In fact, later, I looked at the sentence I'd been working on and had stopped when the call had interrupted me. It was the sentence that reads: "What am I supposed *to* learn from these Christian signs of an afterlife associated with Mickey?" The cursor was blinking at me from within the word "to", flashing at me from its location nestled between the "t" and the "o".

It appeared like this: t|o

You might say the cursor stopped between a cross and a zero. This symbolically represents what I thought was the reason I found the cross—to change the "1" on Mickey's gravestone to a "0". But this new message came from Mark, and his concern was that I get right with Jesus. Perhaps the blinking cursor represents a body, "alive" and blinking, on the cross, further emphasizing Mark's suggestion that the cross is actually a crucifix.

That is synchronicity, and for me it further indicates communication between this realm of existence and another. It's as if, before he left this life, my brother Mark tried to tell me, again, to pay attention.

I wish I knew why I get these messages. I don't know why, and I'm not about to start a religion over them. I just wish someone could tell me what I am supposed to do with this information besides tell my family and put it in this book. Then again, maybe that's what I am supposed to do—and that is that.

RESOURCES

The following resources may prove helpful to family members of murder victims.

RESOURCES FOR FAMILIES OF MURDER VICTIMS

Anti-Violence Partnership www.avpphila.org/links.html
Families of Murder Victims www.avpphila.org/fmv.html
Murder Victims.com http://www.murdervictims.com/
Murder Victims' Families
www.murdervictimsfamilies.org
National Center for Victims of Crime www.ncvc.org
National Organization for Victim Assistance
www.trynova.org/
National Organization of Parents of Murdered Children,
Inc. www.pomc.com
Office for Victims of Crime www.ojp.usdoj.gov/ovc
Parents of Murdered Children www.pomc.org

ORGANIZATIONS FOR ABOLITION OF THE DEATH PENALTY

Amnesty International USA
www.amnestyusa.org/death-penalty

DPIC Death Penalty Information Center
www.deathpenaltyinfo.org
MADP Missourians for Alternatives to the Death Penalty
www.madpmo.org
MVFR Murder Victims' Families for Reconciliation
www.mvfr.org
NCADP National Coalition to Abolish the Death Penalty
www.ncadp.org
New Yorkers Against the Death Penalty www.nyadp.org
Ohioans to Stop Executions www.otse.org
Death Penalty Focus
https://death.rdsecure.org/index.php
Stop Capital Punishment Now
www.stopcapitalpunishment.org/abolitionist.html

Made in the USA
Middletown, DE
04 December 2018